D0461730

WRITING FOR
DECISION MAKERS

WRITING FOR DECISION MAKERS

Memos and Reports with a Competitive Edge

Marya W. Holcombe and Judith K. Stein

 Lifetime Learning Publications
Belmont, California
A division of Wadsworth, Inc.

Developmental Editor: Marty Carpenter
Text Designer: Diane Hoyt-Goldsmith

Printed in the United States of America

2 3 4 5 6 7 8 9 10—85 84 83 82 81

Library of Congress Cataloging in Publication Data

Holcombe, Marya, 1944–
    Writing for decision makers.

    Bibliography
  1. Business report writing. I. Stein, Judith,
1935–   joint author. II. Title.
HF5719.H64   808′.066658021   80-24900
ISBN 0-534-97980-7

CONTENTS

6 | Beginnings and Endings: What, Why, and How   85

Beginnings: attracting the reader's attention; providing just enough information; establishing rapport with the reader. Endings: providing a sense of closure; summarizing; setting out the next step.

7 | Writing the First Draft   101

Choosing a format: modified outline versus prose format; how to present a long report. Beginning to write; how to keep going; setting manageable goals; picking the right method. Where to begin. Guidelines for first drafts.

8 | Design for Emphasis   117

Designing the report or memo: reinforcing the main points; helping the reader follow the argument; making it attractive. Constructing visuals: use tables and charts intelligently; choose an appropriate visual form; evaluate your tables and charts.

9 | Revising is Quality Control   143

Revising for organization. Revising for language: use language assertively; construct sentences to show relationships; say what you mean; choose words that work for you; use an appropriate tone; avoid sexist language. Proofread your memo or report.

10 | Helping Others Write Effectively   163

Guidelines for appraising writing. Reviewing the writing of your peers and subordinates. Reviewing for superiors.

Appendixes   173

Acknowledgements

In writing this book we were helped and encouraged by a great many people who listened to our ideas and gave us the benefit of their thinking. Foremost among these is Larry Isaacson, who pushed us to think harder, played devil's advocate, and considered new ideas with us. We would also like to thank Dennis Perkins for his insights and support during the writing process. In addition, we are especially grateful to those managers who jeopardized old friendships by honestly giving us their thoughts on early versions of this book: Art Bulger, Earle Kazis, Alan Koss and Dave Kramer. We are pleased that those friendships remain intact, just as we are pleased that our secretary, Karyn Rapuano, has survived countless drafts and is still with us. Any errors or misinterpretations, of course, are ours alone.

We are also grateful to those students and managers who shared their reports and memos with us, providing material on which the examples in this book are based. The data for the Budget Finance Corporation case were kindly provided by Stanley Kanney. The information is accurate; the names of people and organizations have been changed. Permission to excerpt from *Investments for a Changing Economy*, August–September 1979, was granted by Merrill Lynch Pierce Fenner and Smith. Permission to excerpt from *New England Business*, July 17, 1979, was granted by the editors.

For my family—Terry, Kerry, and Brette; Mom, Dad, and Rae Ann.
M.W.H.

To Mike, for his support and understanding,
and to Jimmy and Roberta, for their good-natured sufferance.
J.K.S.

Preface

Demands on your time as a manager are endless, and you're often competing with others for support for your plans, ideas, and objectives. You realize that writing quickly, efficiently, and forcefully is essential to making the best use of your time and gaining that support. So you've picked up this book—a bit skeptically, because you've tried others with similar titles, and they've offered you only a rehash of eighth-grade grammar and a few hints about creativity and outlining. *This book is different.* We wrote it because we feel that by applying the managerial skills you already have to your writing, you can improve your reports and memos almost instantly and gain the competitive edge you need.

You will find very little grammar in this book. Instead, we show you how to plan, organize, and present your thoughts on paper in a way that will produce results. Each chapter tells you how to attack a step in the writing process:

- Identifying and focusing on the reader
- Solving the problem
- Planning your argument and drawing a picture of it
- Writing exciting and useful beginnings and endings
- Writing the first draft
- Adding visuals
- Revising
- Making the document attractive

There is also a unique chapter on helping others to write better by effectively appraising their writing, and on editing and reviewing for superiors, sensitive tasks often neglected in management writing books.

We've included dozens of examples of managers' writing to show you the improvements that result when our techniques are applied. Checklists and guidelines will enable you to recognize and remedy your own particular writing weaknesses. You'll find that once you've learned a few simple rules, you can use this system for any kind of writing you do on the job—letters, memos, reports, and speeches. We are convinced that reading this book and practicing its lessons will prove to you that good managerial writing is not an inborn talent, but a skill that can be learned and put to your competitive advantage.

Marya W. Holcombe
Judith K. Stein

1

THE MANAGERIAL APPROACH TO WRITING

"Your writing tells a reader whether you are bright or dull, prepared or lazy, precise or sloppy. It is even more important than the way you act or dress."

"It's harder to waffle on paper—what you write is like a window into your mind."

We're sure you've read or heard hundreds of statements like these, made by senior executives of national corporations. Our purpose is not to preach, once again, that writing is important; you already know that. We've written this book because writing is a process, like any other management process, and we want to show you some steps you can take to write more efficiently and effectively.

What This Book Can Do for You

Many bright and capable managers go to great lengths to avoid writing. Perhaps you're one of them. Do you regularly call people rather than write a memo or letter explaining your position? Do you feel that writing makes you and your ideas vulnerable? You're not alone. We've taught hundreds of executives with precisely these attitudes. We don't promise quick and easy tricks to better writing. And we're not from the "writing is fun" school. Writing well is hard work. Nevertheless, if you learn how to apply your managerial skills to problem solving and to organizing and writing reports and memos, your communications will improve almost immediately. By the time you finish chapter 10, you will be producing more convincing memos and reports and you'll also be getting them done less painfully.

Take Stock of the Skills You Already Have

The skills you have developed for doing your job well—dealing with people, confronting problems, planning for action, marketing a product, checking product quality—can be tapped to write more effective memos and reports.

Managers deal with people. As a manager, you probably spend a good deal of time coaching your subordinates and an equal amount of time listening to your superior's objectives and meshing them with your own. When you write, use your skills with people to meet the needs of a specific reader, the person who will take action.

Managers are problem solvers. You can adapt your problem solving skills to analyze the problem from the reader's perspective, establish criteria, generate solutions, and determine feasibility.

Managers are planners. You wouldn't think of undertaking a complex project without a plan. Make sure you don't grab a pencil or reach for a dictating machine unless you've organized your thoughts and diagrammed your *writing* plan.

Managers are marketing people. Ideas, and arguments, like other products, are useless if you don't market them. You can use your marketing creativity to target your message to the right reader.

Managers are concerned with quality control. No production manager would ship anything—from a transistor to a tank—without checking its quality. You can learn revision skills that will insure that your writing products are of uniformly high quality.

All these managerial skills can help produce memos and reports that get action. This book will show you how.

How to Use This Book

Although writing is not a strictly linear process (as you write, you frequently backtrack and make changes or discover a new approach and revise accordingly), reading the chapters of this book in sequence is the most effective way to master the process itself. We begin with the reader, without whom there would be no memo or report, and demonstrate techniques for defining the problem from the reader's perspective. The middle chapters give you help in learning to solve the problem, group and order ideas to persuade the reader, and check the logic of the argument. When you are ready to write, later chapters tell you how to construct an effective beginning, write a first draft, and revise the memo or report. Most steps build on the preceding ones—if you've correctly identified and analyzed your primary reader, for example, you'll be able to do better problem solving.

However, you may choose to start with a chapter that deals with a particular difficulty you have and master that chapter first. Many managers find this a motivating approach because they see immediate improvement in an aspect of writing that has given them trouble.

To decide what parts of the writing process are most difficult for you, do a little brainstorming. What frustrates you most? Is it finding the right words to introduce your subject? Is it making your points in an order that is both logical and persuasive? Jot down these general concerns. Now take two or three memos you've written recently, preferably short ones (one to two pages is a good length). Answer the questions on the Writing Checklist for each memo.

Writing Checklist

		Yes	No	Not Sure
1.	Who will take action on the basis of this memo? Is the memo written to convince the primary reader?	_____	_____	_____
2.	Is it clear *why* you are writing?	_____	_____	_____
3.	Do you tell the reader, within the first few sentences, the one major point and the supporting points you intend to make?	_____	_____	_____
4.	Do you limit your discussion to those points?	_____	_____	_____
5.	Do you answer the questions that are likely to come to the reader's mind when he or she reads the memo? These are likely to be questions beginning with "how" or "why."	_____	_____	_____
6.	Have you grouped your supporting ideas in a way that makes the fewest, most significant points?	_____	_____	_____
7.	Do you make the same point only once?	_____	_____	_____
8.	Do you make your points in the most convincing order?	_____	_____	_____
9.	Is it clear what *action* the reader should take?	_____	_____	_____
10.	Are the major points identified visually for the reader?	_____	_____	_____
11.	Is it clear what point is being illustrated by each exhibit?	_____	_____	_____
12.	Is your grammar correct? Does the memo read smoothly?	_____	_____	_____

Your answers will provide a clue to the areas in which your writing needs improvement. In fact, if you had to leave some blank because you weren't quite sure what we were asking for, it's a good indication that you've identified an area in which you need work. The following list guides you to the chapters that offer help with specific trouble spots, and you may want to spend more time on those chapters. If a chapter covers something you already know (you've never had any problems constructing exhibits, for example), you may want to skim it.

Question 1: Who will take action on the basis of this memo? Chapter 2, *Right Reader—Right Information,* will help you identify the reader and provide the information he or she needs.

Is the memo written to convince the primary reader? Chapter 2, chapter 4, *Structuring Your Writing,* chapter 7, *Writing the First Draft,* and chapter 9, *Revising Is Quality Control,* provide guidelines for adopting the appropriate approach.

Questions 2 and 3: Is it clear *why* you are writing? Do you tell the reader, within the first few sentences, the one major point and the supporting points you intend to make? Chapter 6, *Beginnings and Endings,* will help you write creative and complete introductions.

Question 4: Do you limit your discussion to the major points? Chapter 4 and chapter 5, *Picturing Your Strategy,* will show you how to organize your ideas and how to check visually that you have not included anything irrelevant.

Question 5: Do you answer all the questions that are likely to come to the reader's mind? Chapter 3, *Getting the Right Information,* offers techniques for checking that you've solved the right problem, included everything important, and considered all the possible alternatives.

Question 6: Have you grouped your supporting ideas in a way that makes the fewest, most significant points? Chapter 4 will help you put your ideas in meaningful categories and make appropriate generalizations about them.

Question 7: Do you make the same point only once? Chapter 5 provides suggestions that will prevent you from repeating yourself. Chapter 9 provides a checklist to guarantee that you will eliminate redundancies in the editing process.

Question 8: Do you make your points in the most convincing order? Chapter 4 has clues to help you use what you know about your audience to select the appropriate order.

Question 9: Is it clear what *action* the reader should take? Chapter 6 describes endings that encourage prompt implementation.

Question 10: Are the major points identified visually for the reader? Chapter 8, *Design for Emphasis,* will show you how to use bullets, caps, underlining, and headings to reinforce your major points.

Question 11: Is it clear what point is being illustrated by each exhibit? Chapter 8 gives models of charts and tables that emphasize special relationships and describes a method for writing effective headings.

Question 12: Is your grammar correct? Does the memo read smoothly? Chapter 9 shows you how to revise for organization and for language.

Of course, identifying the writing skills you need to work on and reading through this book is easier than applying what you've learned. We debated whether to include exercises. After all, most busy managers ignore exercises—they prefer to use their energy for something real. We finally decided that a case study approach would provide you with a realistic opportunity to apply what you've learned as you master each part of the book.

Using the Cases and Exercises

The end-of-the-chapter exercises are based on the two cases in Appendix 1. These cases, which are similar to those used in many business schools, describe the experiences of *real* people facing *real* problems.

The Complex Assembly Corporation case deals with an ethical problem. The chief engineer of an aerospace company, who has been presented with evidence that test results have been tampered with, must explain his decision to top management and to the engineer who brought the irregularity to his attention. No mathematical calculations are required to do this case. In the Budget Finance Corporation case, a loan officer must make a recommendation to the bank's finance committee concerning a loan. Although financial data are provided, you don't have to use them in preparing the case. You should read quickly through both cases and choose the one that appeals to you. If you have time, doing the exercises for both will give you additional practice.

Appendix 2 contains two approaches to answering each exercise. After you have done the exercises for each chapter, comparing your responses with those in this appendix will help you judge and sharpen your skills. Remember, as you look at the examples, that there are no "right" answers in management writing—just more or less effective approaches.

Many management writing books say you can only improve your writing by practice, practice, practice. We believe that you'll learn more by doing these exercises than by writing twenty practice memos a week.

Setting Your Own Goals

To determine your writing goals, you should:
- Describe what you should be able to do
- Outline the conditions under which you should be able to do it

You should base your goals on the chapters in the book. For example, after you finish reading chapter 2 you might think about this goal:

> By the time I finish doing the exercise in chapter 2, I should be able to identify the reader before I write and to phrase the most important question that reader might ask about the subject of the memo.

If you tie your goals to on-the-job opportunities to apply them, you'll be able to see improvement almost immediately. But don't just concentrate on the here and now. Also keep in mind that the skills you are learning will pay even bigger bonuses as your career advances. And that is the whole point behind this book—to help you do your job better now and to get ahead in the future.

2
RIGHT READER—
RIGHT INFORMATION

Identifying and learning about your primary reader will help you know:
- How to respond to the reader's question
- How to avoid writing unnecessarily
- How to provide the information the reader needs
- How to use an appropriate style

Management writing is pragmatic. Managers write because information must be clearly transmitted to someone who needs to act on a problem or opportunity. You write to superiors to explain some action you have taken or to provide information on which they or someone else may act. You write to subordinates to explain a new procedure or policy because they need the information to do their jobs. Even when you write to create a record, you establish a history that precludes unnecessary or repetitive actions.

Identify the Primary Reader

To determine the primary reader, then, ask yourself this question: *Who will take action on the basis of this memo or report?* Usually, you can answer this quickly, particularly if you are initiating the communication. You know what results you want and who will act. When a superior asks you to write, however, the primary reader of the communication may be less obvious. The report or memo may be passed along to someone else, or it may go out over another person's signature. If you're not sure what will happen to a communication, you should ask. If the head of your division wants you to summarize the company's available alternatives in response to declining sales in men's cologne, for instance, it's quite likely that the vice-president for sales will take the lead in deciding on a course of action. If so, the vice-president is your primary reader, and the one person whose needs you *must* meet. However, if a committee of the board of directors wants the information, the scope of the report may be very different. Occasionally, the most important reader may be someone totally unexpected, a corporate attorney, a member of the accounting staff, or a union representative who may dispute the action you're writing about— a dismissal, for example. The key question is, who will take action?

Respond to the Reader's Question

To provide necessary and correct information to the primary reader, you must first view the problem from that reader's perspective. One of the most common complaints from managers is that the reports they receive frequently deal with the wrong problem, too large a problem, or no problem at all. The best way to be sure you are addressing the correct problem is to *phrase it in the form of a question that might arise in the reader's mind.* Most often, this ques-

tion will be some form of, "What action should I take to . . . ?"
or, "Why should I . . . ?" Putting the problem in the form of a
question is equally important whether you are writing at someone's request or initiating the communication.

When Someone Requests That You Write

When you are asked to write a report or memo, you can often
turn the request into a question without asking for any clarifi-
cation. If your boss says, "Give me a memo on the affirmative
action meeting," it is safe to assume that he or she wants to know,
"What action do I have to take as a result of the meeting?" or,
"In what ways will the decisions made at the meeting affect my
department?"

Frequently, though, managers don't give precise assignments,
sometimes because they haven't thought a problem through and
sometimes because they assume that you know what they want.
Don't be afraid to ask questions to get the information you need.

If the request was vague, and you can't question the person
directly, you'll have to sift through the clues you have. If someone
has asked you for an evaluation of the public relations department,
it's likely that something has happened recently to spark interest
in that department. Ask around. You may find that the company's
image was severely tarnished because the public relations people
put out contradictory news releases about chemical contamination
of the water table in the vicinity of one of your larger plants. In
that case, the question you'll have to answer—the central idea of
your memo—will be, "What action can we take to improve the
department's coordination on release of sensitive material?" If you
find the public relations department is under fire for some other
reason—the president objected to the design of the annual report,
for example—you'll be answering a different question.

Whenever possible, once you think you have correctly worded
the question, you should go to the primary reader and ask, "If I
answer this question, will you have all the information you need?"
It is an inexcusable waste of time to write a report or memo that
answers the wrong question or answers the right one inadequately.

When You Initiate the Communication

When you write at someone else's request, that person knows
your purpose. When you initiate a communication, the reader has
no way of knowing what your purpose is. In this case, it is particularly important to word the problem as a question the reader

might ask. After all, you have been thinking about the problem for some time and you have a great deal you could say about it. You may easily say too much or not provide the proper guidelines.

Suppose that you are a manager for a soft-drink bottling company. You fondly remember the soft drink of your childhood in Maine. You have developed an extract that closely resembles the original flavor, and you want to tell the president of the company about your idea. If you define your task as writing a memo to "tell the CEO about my idea," you might begin the memo,

> When camping in the Maine woods last summer I had a terrific idea. There was a soft drink around when I was growing up that has been off the market for years. I came back and spent three months developing an extract that is close to the flavor of the drink I remember. Everyone in my department has tasted it and likes it. They think we can really find a market for it . . .

Seem foolish? Many memos begin this way. They tell the reader how the writer came upon the idea, what work has been done and, if the reader is lucky, what the writer has found. The reader, on the other hand, has other needs. He or she is likely to be less interested in the genesis and development of the idea than in its value. Why should we produce this new drink? You might start the soft drink memo this way:

> Market research shows a strong consumer demand for products with flavors reminiscent of "the good old days." We can take advantage of this demand to increase our market share in soft drinks. Our new-products department has developed a flavor similar to that of a popular drink of the '40s. With it we should be able to take advantage of a growing New England market . . .

Phrasing the problem as a question the reader might ask allows you to set appropriate boundaries for the discussion and guarantees that you leave out nothing important.

When you write to explain a decision to subordinates, you also need to see the problem, opportunity, or decision from the reader's perspective. The subordinate wants to know the same thing your boss wants to know: "What action will I have to take on the basis of this memo or report?" Of course, in this case the decision has already been made or the policy or procedure has already been adopted. The subordinate still has to know what to do as a result of the decision and whether there will be any indirect consequences. The question, and therefore the focus of the report or memo, must be, "What does this have to do with me?" Subordinates have a right to know why you took the action, too. But you'll simply describe your reasons in general terms rather than justify them as you must when you're writing to superiors.

> *Take a few of your most recent memos or reports and answer the following questions about each:*
> - *Who is the primary reader?*
> - *What is the question the reader might ask?*
> - *Does the report or memo meet the test of answering the reader's question?*

If you have consistently answered *yes* to the last question, you are probably a pretty good writer. If not, you are not alone. Focusing on the primary reader and the question that reader wants answered will instantly improve your next memo or report.

Avoid Unnecessary Communication

Knowing your reader and the question you want to answer will also help you avoid writing unnecessarily. Executives moan about the proliferation of paper in their organizations. Unnecessary writing is expensive, and the likelihood that an important message will get lost increases as the pile of paper on any manager's desk grows higher. Moreover, constructing a clear and persuasive memo or report takes time and energy. Unless you've been asked to write, try not to invest your energy in a lost cause. Consider whether your primary reader will act on your message and, if so, whether writing is the best way to communicate.

There are times you should not communicate at all:
- The reader doesn't have the resources to act on your recommendation. If your department's budget has been cut by 15 percent, your boss won't buy your suggestion about instituting merit pay increases to raise morale no matter how well you write the memo.
- The reader is busy dealing with a crisis. Frequently, the idea is good but the timing is poor. If that is the case, save the memo for a more opportune occasion.
- There is nothing to act on. Many memos are self-serving. If no one needs the information, you should forget about writing.

Even if you have an appropriate message and the right audience for it, writing may not be the best way to accomplish your objective. You may be able to inform or persuade the potential reader simply by telephoning or setting up a quick meeting.

Is This Memo Necessary?

To determine whether you should write, ask yourself these questions:
1. Is the problem so complex or technical that it will be better understood in writing?
2. Is my relationship with the reader too formal to make a phone call?
3. Do I need a permanent record of the communication?
4. Will the reader keep the memo or report as a reminder or a reference?
5. Is this the only way I can reach this person?

If you do decide to write, keeping a specific person or group in mind will help you limit the number of people who receive copies. The office copier has turned far too many managers into direct-mail specialists. When everyone gets a copy of everything, you waste everybody's time. It's legitimate to make sure people have the information they need to do their jobs well, but deluging them with memos they do not need is self-defeating. If you send people only important communications, they will treat anything they receive from you with respect.

Understand the Primary Reader

Now that you have determined that a written communication is necessary, you should begin to make notes to help you shape your next memo or report. For an informal memo it is probably enough to jot down the primary reader's name and organizational position, the question the reader might ask, and any preconceived ideas he or she has about the problem. For a formal report you might want to fill out a form like the one on the next page and keep it on your desk as you write.

Reader Guideline

Subject of the report or memo:

Name of the primary reader:

Question the reader might ask:

My position in relation to the primary reader:
  —professional:
  —personal:

How extensive is his or her knowledge of the subject?
  (great, minimal, nonexistent—describe)

What are his or her biases or preconceived ideas about the
  subject?

What are his or her significant managerial traits and stylistic
  preferences?

Who are the secondary readers?

Is anyone else likely to receive this report?

This guideline covers points that will be discussed more fully in
the rest of the chapter. If you are currently working on a writing
project, you'll find the guideline is a handy tool to start using right
away.

Why is it so hard to write a report or memo when it is so easy to
write a letter to a good friend? For one thing, you're not worried
about the impression you will make on your friend. For another,
you know how much information your friend needs, what preconceived ideas he or she has about a subject, and what style of writing or language is acceptable. If you and your friend are engineers, you may write about a project using technical language. If
you are public relations experts, you will describe the project in
other terms. If you know your friend is opposed to the project you
have just undertaken, you may want to explain fully your reasons

for your position. If he or she is offended by slang, you won't use it. In other words, the more you know about your reader, the easier it is for you to write convincingly.

The same argument applies in writing reports and memos. You have an idea you want the reader to understand. You convert that idea into words; the reader looks at the words, decodes them, and converts them back into a concept. If your reader misinterprets your meaning or arrives at a different concept, communication will break down. This occurs daily. Readers frequently misunderstand when their perception of the world differs from the writer's. Suppose your primary reader comes from a different cultural background and is much older than you are. To you, "institutional loyalty" means doing the best job you can for the company or agency while you're there, with an eye to the next job somewhere else. To the reader, "institutional loyalty" means total commitment to the institution for the foreseeable future. A lack of sensitivity to such a difference can result in a report that is misunderstood, is not understood at all, or offends the reader.

In finding out as much as possible about your primary reader, your goal is not to "tell him what he wants to hear." Instead, it is to help you set boundaries for the discussion, to provide enough but no more information and supporting data than is necessary for the reader to understand and be persuaded by the argument. Knowing about the reader also minimizes the possibility that you will unintentionally offend by your choice of language or format.

To make your writing more useful to your primary reader, you should learn what you can about his or her:
- Knowledge of the field
- Preconceptions and biases about the subject
- Style of dealing with people and problems

The Reader's Knowledge of the Subject

Finding out what the reader does or doesn't know will keep you from underexplaining or overexplaining. If an accountant needs technical information about a process to understand why your costs are high, you must be able to provide a convincing and thorough explanation. In contrast, if your boss receives an inflated report rehashing old information rather than supplying new solutions, you may be in trouble. In one case we studied, an executive vice-president asked his assistant to review five locations for a new plant proposed by an outside real-estate consultant. The assistant began by reviewing the alternatives in detail: the location and size of each site, the power sources, the neighborhood. In fact, he repeated a good deal of the consultant's report. When the vice-president got to page 4, he called the assistant in and said, "I want to know what *you* think of these alternatives. If I don't remember the specifics, I can look them up or call the consultant. I don't pay you to be a parrot."

The Reader's Preconceptions and Biases

Case 1: Roy Jones, the head of a manufacturing division of a large conglomerate, found a factory that he was anxious to buy. He developed a long report, including reams of statistical data. Jones was particularly pleased because he calculated that the return on investment would be better than 10 percent in the first year. He began the executive summary this way:

> The Baxter Property presents a particularly attractive opportunity to expand our small-engine production. We can purchase the factory for $500,000 and we should net $55,000 in the first year, thus realizing a return on investment of better than 10 percent.

The president of the company, however, was more interested in how soon he could increase his engine production than he was in the return on the investment in this one plant. He read the first paragraph of the memo and wrote back, "When can we be in operation?" If Jones had considered the president's bias, he might have begun the memo this way:

> If we purchase the Baxter property, we can be in operation in five months and we'll be able to fill our current backlog of purchase orders by January. The attractive price of the plant, as well as its production capabilities, should permit us to realize a better than 10 percent return on investment next year.

Case 2: Your boss is concerned because productivity is suffering in your department. In his view, people are basically lazy and do only as much as they have to do. He feels that the way to improve productivity is to institute stricter controls so you can identify the malingerers and freeze them out during the next round of promotions and raises. You feel, however, that productivity is declining because many of the workers are new on the job and simply haven't yet acquired the skills to do their jobs well. Obviously, you won't get the best results by confronting the boss head-on or by criticizing his opinions. Instead, focus on the objective—increasing productivity. Gather information from other departments or organizations that supports a recommendation for the introduction of training programs. You may ultimately be able to convince the boss that training workers adequately reduces employee turnover and increases productivity.

Case 3: In a study discussed by Fleishman and Bass *(Studies in Personnel and Industrial Psychology,* 1974), executives were asked to read a company case history and to identify the company's chief problem. The researchers found that "although each person read the same factual material, the particular problem identified (such as sales, human relations, or production) depended on the executive's own specialty." If your background is different from your reader's—he's a personnel specialist and you're in production, for example—force yourself to look at the issue from his point of view. If you're recommending a change in the production system to make it more efficient, and you want the personnel manager on your side, avoid suggestions that will disrupt informal work groups or otherwise antagonize employees.

In each of these cases, sensitivity to others' biases or preconceptions is of prime importance. Paying attention to your reader's concerns will not only make your writing more effective, but may also help you solve problems more creatively or foresee unanticipated consequences.

The Reader's Style of Dealing with People and Problems

As you know, managers have vastly different styles of dealing with people, problems, and opportunities. Sometimes your reader's style may clash with your own. Once again, the solution is not to turn chameleon. But, by being aware of the reader's style, you may be able to adjust your writing to avoid unnecessary conflict and hard feelings.

Formal versus informal. An authoritarian or old-fashioned boss may view a memo written in the first person *(I, we)* as presumptuous and too familiar. On the other hand, using exaggerated formality in messages to subordinates may create the impression that you're cold and unapproachable. If your memos to subordinates sound like orders from a three-star general to a backward corporal, your staff will be resentful—and you may never know why. Sometimes you have to deal with a reader's whims or perception of the organization's image as well. One sales manager consistently returned letters his salespeople wrote with the comment, "too folksy," even though the salespeople had established friendly relationships with their customers. In response, the salespeople learned to humanize their communications without resorting to the first person.

Advice versus evaluation. Some executives object to receiving a recommendation memo that fails to give all the serious alternatives and the arguments for and against them. They feel the decisions are theirs to make, not the writer's. Managers who write to such executives have to take care to state all the important criteria and discuss the alternatives at length.

High-context versus low-context. Some managers consider anything but the barest explanation superfluous, and more than one or two exhibits turn them off. One vice-president we know rips the top page off every memo or report that he finds in his in-basket and sends the rest back to the writer. If the writer has waited until page 3 to reveal the main point, this vice-president will never see it. At the other extreme are managers who want all the available data to judge the quality of the argument. Unless you're dealing with an exaggerated version of either type, try to strike a balance. One manager complained, "Everything I get is so wordy as to be incomprehensible or so terse as to be impolite." Strive for a memo or report that's somewhere in between.

> *In reviewing your recent writing, have you considered:*
> - *The reader's level of knowledge about the subject?*
> - *Any preconceived ideas that might serve as barriers to understanding?*
> - *Anything about the reader's style of dealing with problems that should influence the content or tone of your communication?*
> - *Whether you know enough about the reader?*

How to Find Out about Your Reader

Usually, just thinking about your reader's preconceptions, knowledge, and style will give you the guidance you need to write responsively. Sometimes, however, when you are writing to someone you don't know well, you want more information. If possible, speak to the primary reader to clarify any questions. If that's not an option, you might ask someone who knows about the person's preferences and background. Education and experience provide clues about the reader's knowledge of the subject and may indicate stylistic preference. We have found that people with academic or scientific/technical backgrounds tend to be process-oriented, preferring an argument that is developed by repeating the writer's thinking process. People with backgrounds in business or law are more interested in answers—they want to know what the writer thinks first and then the support for that conclusion. Looking over some memos or reports your potential reader has written may also provide useful clues. If these communications are flawless, try to make your writing equally impeccable. But even if the memos and reports are a slapdash combination of unrelated thoughts, don't jump to the conclusion that you have been given carte blanche to write badly. No matter how they write, most executives can recognize and prefer to receive well-written reports.

SUMMARY

When you prepare to write, for better results you should:
- Identify the primary reader for this specific memo or report by asking who will take action on it
- State the subject of the report or memo as a question the primary reader might ask
- Decide whether you should be writing at all and eliminate any unnecessary secondary readers
- Find out as much as possible about your reader's
  —knowledge of the topic
  —preconceptions and biases
  —style in dealing with problems and people
- Learn about the reader to determine
  —the scope of the memo or report
  —its organization
  —its length
  —its tone or style

Case Study Exercises

In the back of the book are two cases. In Budget Finance Corporation the memo is clearly directed to the bank investment committee. In Complex Assembly Corporation the content and tone of the memorandum will be quite different depending on the reader.

1. **Complex.** If you choose Complex Assembly, fill in the Reader Guideline given below assuming you are Russo writing to explain your decision to (a) top management or (b) Sam Pilawski.

2. **Budget.** If you choose Budget, fill in the form as if you are writing to the bank's investment committee.

Reader Guideline

Subject of the report or memo:

Name of the primary reader:

Question the reader might ask:

My position in relation to the primary reader:
   —professional:
   —personal:

How extensive is his or her knowledge of the subject?
   (great, minimal, nonexistent—describe)

What are his or her biases or preconceived ideas about the subject?

What are his or her significant managerial traits and stylistic preferences?

Who are the secondary readers?

Is anyone else likely to receive this report?

<u>Reminder:</u> Although "answers" to chapter exercises are provided for each case study, you will benefit most from working through each exercise and developing your own solutions. Keep in mind that there are really no right or wrong answers. Finally, compare your solutions to those in Appendix 2.

Further References

Boettinger, Henry M. *Moving Mountains: The Art and Craft of Letting Others See Things Your Way.* New York: Macmillan, 1969.
A good introduction to persuasive techniques and ways to analyze your audience or reader for all sorts of presentations—memos, reports, and speeches.

Gemmill, Gary. "Managing Upward Communication," *Personnel Journal* (February, 1970).
Although this short article lacks the pithy examples that would make it most useful, it provides insight into a common management dilemma.

Rogers, Carl R. and Roethlisberger, F. J. "Barriers and Gateways to Communication," *Harvard Business Review* (July–August, 1952).
A still current and valuable description of the way barriers to communication actually operate in business. Required reading for those who have just begun to think about identifying the reader.

Shurter, Robert L., Williamson, J. Peter, and Broehl, Wayne G., Jr. *Business Research and Report Writing.* New York: McGraw-Hill, 1965.
Chapter 4's first few pages expand on the techniques outlined in this chapter.

3

GETTING THE RIGHT ANSWER

Problem solving is a three-step process. This chapter will show you:

- How to analyze and research the problem
- How to establish criteria that measure how well alternatives meet objectives
- How to evaluate and choose among alternatives

"My people don't write clearly because they solve problems hap-hazardly." In our interviews with executives and managers, comments like this cropped up repeatedly. To these men and women, proper problem solving meant analyzing a situation to find the parts or the cause of the problem, evaluating alternatives, and making realistic recommendations. Truly creative managers follow a carefully structured system to be sure that they leave out nothing important. This chapter outlines that system. It's challenging, but, if you master it, you will avoid wasting time on unnecessary research and will produce clearer and more coherent reports.

Whether you are writing because you discovered a problem yourself or because someone has asked you for information, you have already posed the problem as a question that might arise in the mind of the reader. No manager needs to be told that it is unwise to simply accept another person's assessment of a situation. Biases and preconceptions may interfere with anyone's ability to determine the real cause of the problem. Your first task as a writer, then, is to make certain that you understand the problem correctly—that you know the cause or have all the parts.

Finding the Real Problem

To be sure you have properly identified the problem, you should analyze it by breaking it into its components, and research it systematically. For simple problems, you can do this in your head; for most, however, writing your analysis down schematically will help you see components and relationships, insuring that you haven't forgotten anything important. Developing a need-to-know list will focus your research.

Useful Tools: Analysis Trees and Flow Charts

Two tested problem solving devices are the analysis tree and the flow chart. An analysis tree allows you to subdivide components into their parts. A flow chart is a convenient way to determine parts of problems that involve processes.

You draw an analysis tree by writing the question on the left of a page and using branches to show the problem's structure. When you already have all the necessary information and are simply describing something, the analysis tree also provides the outline for your memo or report. This tool is particularly useful in deciding what to write and how to organize your information. In one case, the senior management of a corporation instituted an incentive program that required managers to meet with employees on a regular basis to discuss performance. Having determined that division supervisors were likely to view the new policy as an unreasonable drain on their time, the personnel director, charged with explaining the policy, drew the analysis tree shown in figure 3.1, basing his categories on the questions the supervisors might ask. He then wrote the memo, using the analysis tree as his outline.

If you have a simple topic, drawing the tree is a way of grouping your ideas. To write, you need only decide on the order (described in chapter 5).

Analysis trees for complex problems. If you are dealing with a complex issue, you'll use the analysis tree to determine the cause of the problem. Although such analysis trees cannot be translated directly into memos or reports, they provide the framework for your research and organization. To draw an analysis tree for a complex problem, begin at the left with the question you must answer to solve the problem, which may be different from the question the reader might ask. In one case, a candy manufacturer who wanted to know what to do about declining profits asked a consultant for help. The consultant, in an attempt to determine the cause of the decline, segmented the category "profits" into two major components, costs and contribution. She then drew the analysis tree shown in figure 3.2. By asking questions about each component, she established the direction for her research and found the components of profits that were not producing the expected results. She then could look for the causes of the deviations and ways to correct them.

Many consultants and high-level managers find that drawing analysis trees helps them narrow the scope of their research. Appendix 3 contains several problems, phrased as questions a reader might ask, and the analysis trees managers drew to analyze those problems. Testing your analyses against theirs will allow you to sharpen your skills at using this tool.

Flow charts and causal chains. Flow charts are most useful in analyzing a process or the development of a situation. The new customer relations director of a major international airline, for instance, asked the head of Lost and Found to review operations in his department and recommend any necessary changes. The head of the department drew the flow chart shown in figure 3.3, which

Figure 3.1
Simple Analysis Tree

Question: What is the new incentive policy?

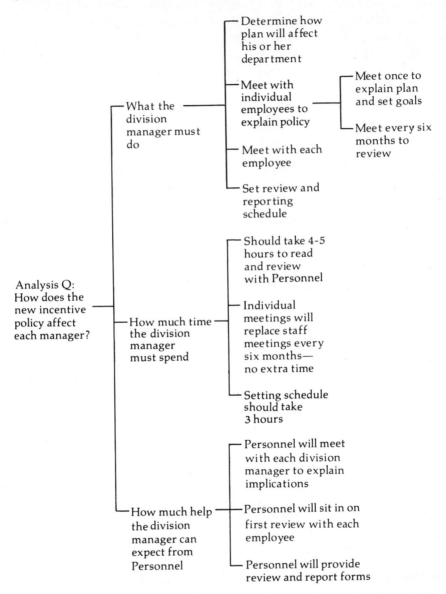

**Figure 3.2
Analysis Tree for Complex Problem**

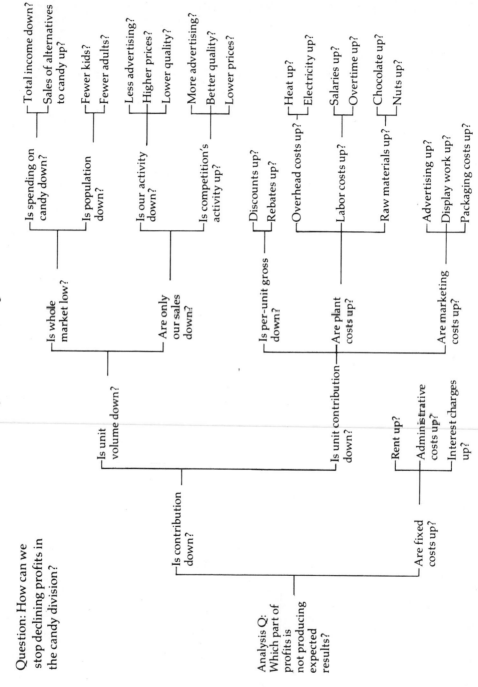

Question: How can we
stop declining profits in
the candy division?

Analysis Q:
Which part of
profits is
not producing
expected
results?

Figure 3.3
Flow Chart

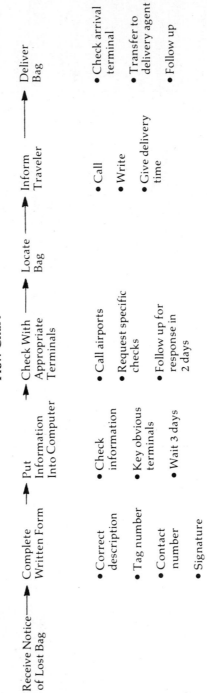

Receive Notice → Complete → Put → Check With → Locate → Inform → Deliver
of Lost Bag   Written Form Information   Appropriate   Bag   Traveler   Bag
                                 Into Computer Terminals

• Correct   • Check   • Call airports   • Call   • Check arrival
  description   information   • Request specific   • Write   terminal

• Tag number   • Key obvious   checks   • Give delivery   • Transfer to
                     terminals   • Follow up for   time   delivery agent
• Contact   response in
  number   • Wait 3 days   2 days   • Follow up

• Signature

he used to develop a series of questions about how the department was functioning.

You can use a flow chart to analyze the development of a situation and to organize a chronologically ordered report. But flow charts as a problem solving device are more often used to determine whether the apparent cause of a problem is the primary cause. Such charts are called "causal chains."

The principals of a law firm, finding that the corporation's net earnings were not keeping pace with its gross income, asked their accountant to find ways to cut costs. The accountant broke the company's expenses into parts and compared each part with county averages. Finding that total clerical costs, as a percentage of gross income, were among the highest in the area, although individual salaries were not above average, he concluded that the office was overstaffed. As a result of his study, several word processors and bookkeepers were replaced with part-time help. Within months, however, the lawyers found overtime costs had escalated and much of the work was poorly done. This time the accountant talked with staff members and determined that some were not working efficiently and that the part-time help was far more costly than full-time help. By changing some jobs and making several part-time positions into one full-time one, he cut costs and improved both the quality of the work and job satisfaction. Although he had correctly broken the whole into parts in the first study, he had not considered the components of salary expense or the environmental factors that affected individuals.

Such superficial acceptance of a cause is not uncommon. After hours or days of work, finding any cause is a great relief. One way to check whether you have found the primary cause is to develop a causal chain and ask yourself, "If I change this, will the desired result always or certainly happen?" Eliminating staff members will not cut expenses if the work cannot be completed by the remaining people.

poor work distribution $\longrightarrow$ overstaffing $\longrightarrow$	high total salaries $\longrightarrow$	low corporate earnings
primary cause *intermediate cause*	*intermediate cause*	*effect*

Often you will want to use an analysis tree or flow chart to find the part of the whole that is malfunctioning and then use the causal chain to be sure that you have the primary cause.

Think about a problem you are working on now. Divide it into its parts by building an analysis tree or by developing a flow chart. Once you know which component is not meeting expectations, build a causal chain. Following this process will increase your understanding of the problem.

The Need-to-Know List: Primary and Secondary Sources

Once you have developed an analysis tree for complex problems, you know what questions you must answer. A need-to-know list based on the questions on the right-hand side of the tree will focus your research and set up a system for getting the answers you need. You may add questions to your need-to-know list as you continue your research and consider alternatives. For long reports, particularly those involving work by several people, the list should include the name of the person responsible for obtaining the information and the date the information is due. The need-to-know list made by the consultant to the candy manufacturer looked in part like this:

Need—to—Know List

Question	Possible Sources	Person Respon- sible	Due Date
Spending on candy down?	Distributors	E.F.	12—1
Candy alternative sales up?	Distributors	E.F.	12—1
	Competitors' annual reports	J.K.	12—4
Candy competitors' sales up?	Competitors' annual reports	J.K.	12—4
New competition?	Distributors	E.F.	12—1

More advertising by competitors?	Marketing man-ager	A.L.	12–1
	Newspapers, TV etc.	J.K.	12–4
	Distributors	E.F.	12–1
Lower wholesale prices offered by competitors?	Distributors	E.F.	12–1
Population down? Where?	Census figures	J.K.	12–4

If you organize your research this way, you won't send people scurrying for unnecessary data. There is nothing so annoying to fellow employees as spending several days finding answers to extraneous questions that the researcher later decides he or she really never needed. If you ask for irrelevant data too often, you'll soon find that people don't return your phone calls.

Getting and organizing information from primary sources. When you list sources on the need-to-know list, remember that your most valuable source of information is other people. An organization is a system made up of complex interrelationships in which much valuable knowledge is never recorded except in the minds of the people who work there. Don't hesitate to ask questions. In seeking the information you need from primary sources, you should keep the following in mind:

- Ask for help and suggestions; people like to be considered experts.
- Consider all sides of the problem, including not only the details on your list, but the context of the organization's objectives and environment as well.
- Seek out both likely and unlikely sources of information: others working on the same problem; predecessors on the job; people with positions similar to yours inside and outside the organization.
- Ask open-ended questions to get all relevant information.
- Ask, "Who else should I talk with?"
- Observe the answerer (not just the answer) for clues to attitudes; observe the situation firsthand if possible.

- For best results, trade information; don't be an interrogator.

Once you've done some fact finding, make sure you store the information appropriately. First, write it down as soon as possible after the meeting. Human memory is notoriously unreliable, and new conversations may cloud your memory of previous talks. Dictating memos for the files is sometimes a useful way to store information, but if you are getting answers for a specific report, you'll be able to retrieve and sort your information more easily if you write it on cards, according to the category you're dealing with.

Here are some simple suggestions for taking notes:

- Put only one important idea on each card.
- Use a number system for sources. Assign a number to each source and write it on a source card, providing enough information to permit you to find the source readily. Then use that number on each research card that provides data from that source.
- File information according to one of the broad categories on the analysis tree.

An information card based on interview data regarding available labor might look like this:

```
3  [key to source]                            Labor Costs

Machinists trained in high school: 2,000 in town
                                   4,000 in sur-
                                      rounding area

Machinists trained in trade           500 in town -
   program:                           all working
                                      for Acme Corp.
                                   1,000 in area
```

During the fact-finding process, someone may have pointed out a factor you hadn't thought of before. For example, you want to franchise your system for computerized diagnosis of car transmission problems. When you ask potential franchisers, you find that they want maintenance as part of the package. When you talk to Louie Dickson, who's in charge of maintenance, you determine that his people are already overburdened and can't be spared to travel to the franchise shops to provide maintenance. You'll then have to go back to your analysis tree and ask questions about the maintenance problem. As you work, you'll add to both your analysis tree and need-to-know list.

Finding and organizing information from secondary sources. Even with reams of printed material at their disposal, managers prefer to deal with firsthand information. But it's a mistake to neglect secondary sources, which provide detailed information about the context in which your organization operates. Aggregate data can help you detect significant variations over time that may allow you to zero in on the problem. If you work for a large corporation, you'll probably have access to a company library. If not, you may already have begun building a reference library. Every field has its own journals and books. Appendix 4 gives a list of some of the most helpful reference sources for managers.

Your company files may provide historical insight; at the least, they may provide clues. Sometimes files reveal information buried so deeply in the past that no one around remembers it. Another source is your own file of relevant articles and clippings. Organize these materials according to appropriate categories for the problems you generally deal with so that you do not find yourself searching aimlessly for a *Fortune* article from last spring that you vaguely remember and believe may help you institute the new budget system. One of the values of such secondary sources is that they frequently suggest useful subcategories you can use to group your own thoughts.

However, don't give in to the primeval urge to collect and massage data endlessly in the hope of finding "something." Think first. If you are concerned with the cost of care at a regional hospital that serves a population of 10,000, for example, knowing the cost of care at Bellevue Hospital in New York City will not help you decide what is appropriate for your hospital. When you made your need-to-know list, you set some limits based on your assessment of the reader's needs. As you do the actual research, try to answer the questions on the list to the most practical level and STOP. If you have done your preparation carefully, and if you don't change your mind about the breadth of the question, you should have enough information.

Once again, use cards to take notes. Be sure to indicate the source so you can double check. For very rich sources, use abbreviations (keep a list so you can remember the abbreviation you use).

Checking for accuracy and usefulness. As you collect information, ask yourself two questions:
● Is it accurate?
● Will it help me solve this problem?
If the answer to either is no, forget that morsel of data, no matter how fascinating. Most people are myopic about their environment, and secondary sources may be biased in some direction. It is your responsibility as a writer-researcher to question every source for accuracy.

Primary and Secondary Source Checklist

Ask yourself these questions about your primary sources:

1. Does the source have a vested interest in the result of the study? Will the results directly affect him or her?

2. Does the source have a reputation for accuracy? (We know some managers whose gift for self-promotion tends to get in the way when they are providing information.)

Ask yourself these questions as you read your secondary sources:

1. Is the source objective? (Are there any obvious biases?)

2. Is the source up-to-date?

3. Are statistical sources comparable? (It may be impossible to use two sets of statistical data to support your argument because they were developed on the basis of different samples or used different methods. Check for this before you actually begin to write your report.)

Once you've found the correct cause, or identified an opportunity and done the appropriate fact finding, you'll be tempted to start proposing solutions. The intervening step, one managers sometimes neglect, is establishing criteria to judge those solutions. Stating and writing down criteria saves you from researching inappropriate alternatives. Also, you will almost always want to include the criteria in the final document. Stating them clearly now means you won't have to write them later.

Establishing Criteria

Criteria are usually set by the report or memo writer. Most often, they are based on corporate goals, the budget, and the specific needs of the person for whom the report or memo is being prepared. For example, if you are suggesting alternative locations for a design showroom, "a rent of no more than $10 a square foot" may be a criterion established by the budget. "A location in midtown" may result from a corporate objective of being readily available to the trade. Simple logistics—the need to exhibit a certain number of pieces of furniture—may dictate the criterion of "2,000 square feet of floor space." "Office space with windows" is a criterion for a manager who gets claustrophobia unless he can see the world outside.

If you've been asked to write, try to find out as much as possible about the objectives of the person who asked you so that you can set appropriate criteria. Don't automatically accept company policies when you are setting criteria. For instance, it may be company policy to send the executive vice-president a copy of every memo written by every staff officer, but if it is your job to recommend ways of cutting down paper shuffling by senior management, that policy should not be a criterion. Policies are often based on generally accepted procedure ("we've always done it this way"). Focus on the underlying objective—in this case, "keeping the executive vice-president informed"—and develop criteria to measure achievement of this objective.

To be useful to the writer in solving the problem and to the reader in understanding the report or memo, criteria must:
- Be stated as standards against which alternatives can be judged
- Be weighted according to importance

Criteria Should Be Stated As Standards

Criteria must indicate the desired outcome and be measurable if they are to be useful in judging alternatives. It is all too easy to jot down "cost" as a criterion because you, as the writer, understand you mean "the lowest cost" or that you cannot exceed your budget of $10,000. Experienced report writers know, however, that it pays to list criteria as declarative statements, such as "cost must not exceed $10,000" or "proposal should increase the candidate's visibility in the northwest suburbs." Writing criteria this way will force you to set precise limits. Avoid confusion by asking yourself, each time you write a criterion, "Will my reader be able to tell how well an alternative meets this standard?" If you have any doubts, define the criterion more precisely.

Criteria fall into two categories: those that must be met and those that are desirable but will be considered in relation to the merits of other criteria. The first group we call *limits of freedom;* the second, *negotiable criteria.* If your project has an absolute maximum cost, such as $5,000, that cost is a limit of freedom. A $6,000 project cannot be considered. If, on the other hand, a negotiable criterion is "the lowest cost," the cost of any alternative will be one of several factors you will consider in judging the relative merits of the alternatives. (Even "a cost of $5,000" may be a negotiable criterion if you have some leeway in spending.) To avoid wasting time on alternatives that exceed your limits of freedom, you should separate those criteria that are limits of freedom from those that are negotiable.

Criteria Should Be Weighted

Once you have established the negotiable criteria, you must make decisions about which are most important. Otherwise, it will be impossible to make any reasonable decision about the alternatives. Weighting criteria is a sophisticated way of ranking them and provides you with a quantitative judgment about your alternatives.

Weighting criteria not only helps you solve the problem, it forces you to formulate and state the reasons for your ranking. You will use these reasons in the final report to support your position. For short memos or uncomplicated problems, it may be enough to rank the criteria in order of their importance with full-sentence statements of your reasons for the ranking. For more complex problems, we suggest you use a numerical scale (1–5 is used frequently in industry). For instance, a manager who was asked to assess the relative merits of three locations to which his company might move its small-parts assembly (see the problem analysis in Appendix 3) decided the relative advantages were based on costs, proximity to the company's primary market, and the availability of labor. He then set these criteria:

Criteria	Weight	Reason
Lowest production cost	2	Costs are less significant than location and labor
Within twelve hours of the major market	5	Our business is based on quick replacement service
Pool of 8,000 skilled workers	3	We need some workers to start but can train high school graduates

Evaluating Alternatives

Unless it's a "go/no go" situation, you have some latitude in developing alternatives to solve the problem or capitalize on an opportunity. If someone specified the alternatives, you are limited. However, if you were asked, "Should we go with the proposed program or scrap it entirely and try something else?" you can play with the "try something else" part to provide sensible alternatives. In this case, you may be able to modify the program in some way without losing your investment. If you're initiating the communication, you can be as creative as you like in generating alternatives, based on the boundaries set by your limits of freedom.

After you have established criteria, spend the first part of your thinking-time just generating alternatives. Save the evaluation for later and don't reject any solution out-of-hand because it seems absurd. Devotion to the status quo can blind you to workable alternatives. Even some that seem ridiculous may be adapted to become workable, or may lead to other ideas.

Assess Alternatives Systematically

Be systematic about assessing the alternatives you've generated. Policy analysts have developed a quantitative technique for assessing alternatives that assigns each alternative a value (on a scale similar to the one used to weight criteria) and multiplies the value by the weight you give the criterion. Using this system, you can develop a picture of how well each alternative meets your criteria. The manager trying to decide on a location for the small-parts assembly plant did it this way:

Criteria	Criteria Weight	Value		Score	Reason for Value	Supporting Data or Chart
		Location A				
Within 12 hours of major market	5	× 5	=	25	10 hours maximum distance	Map
Pool of 8,000 skilled workers	3	5	=	15	10,000 potential workers ages 20–65	Table of population by age and training
Lowest production costs	2	1	=	2	Most expensive location	Table of fixed and variable costs
		TOTAL SCORE		42		
		Location B				
Within 12 hours of major market	5	× 1	=	5	15 hours from market	Map
Pool of 8,000 skilled workers	3	3	=	9	7,000 potential workers	Table
Lowest production costs	2	5	=	10	Least expensive location	Table
		TOTAL SCORE		24		

This formal assessment provided the manager with a "score" for judging each alternative against the others. It also gave him a list of the supporting data he needed. When he sat down to write the first draft of the report, his supporting assertions (reasons) were already on paper. Using a structured alternative assessment allowed him to organize his thinking and save writing time.

If you find the quantitative approach restricting, listing the pros and cons for each alternative, based on the criteria, is another way to visualize the tradeoffs you make in choosing a solution. Whichever approach you take, the point is to (1) apply management skills to assessing alternatives; (2) get supporting evidence on paper in preparation for writing the final report.

Writing Useful Action Plans

Action plans provide options for meeting specific objectives. The careful manager chooses a number of plans which can be considered as a group, allowing coherent reconciliation of conflicts. Action plans, therefore, should be written in a way that invites comparison. Each plan should include the following elements:
- A brief description of the plan in terms of how it meets one or more of the criteria
- What the cost will be
- What the benefits will be

For purposes of organizing your ideas, you may want to use forms like those in the examples below, developed by the fund-raising director of a nonprofit organization. Because he had written out this information as he worked through the problem, when he developed the final report the director needed only to add the name of the person responsible and the starting and completion dates for the plans he recommended.

Action	Expected Results	Support	Cost
Extend mailing to 10,000 potential new donors.	500 contributions of over $25.	Competition gets 5 percent return on similar mailing. Assume the same return.	$5,000

```
Increase staff    $75,000 in    After ground    $25,000
to include two    year two.     breaking pe-
full-time                       riod each
callers.                        caller should
                                produce three
                                times salary.
```

You may prefer to set up action programs so that each is on a separate page, like this:

```
Action:
  Extend mailing to 10,000 potential donors.

Expected Results:
  $12,500

Support:
  Competition gets 5 percent return on mailing. We
should do as well.

Cost:
  $5,000

Drawbacks:
  Limited mailing list.
```

Stating the action plans in either of these ways will enable you to compare programs and develop a plan that will meet your goals. As a bonus, you will have a substantial part of the report in final form before you actually start to write.

Reviewing the Feasibility of Your Solution

Feasibility is actually a limit of freedom. Even if the alternative meets every other criterion for achieving your objective, if you can't make it workable, you'll have to discard it. But because feasibility, in the broad sense, relates to the way your organization works as a system, it's hard to factor in feasibility, particularly for action plans, until you can look at the whole recommendation. Changes in one part of the system affect other parts; it's your job to foresee negative consequences before you adopt any alternative. To test your solution for feasibility, use this checklist, which is loosely adapted from a series in J. R. Hackman and G. R. Oldham, *Word Redesign* (1979):

Feasibility Checklist

1. Does existing technology support this proposal?

2. Will the people involved accept this change?
   —your superior
   —your peers
   —your subordinate

3. Can the organization's existing systems handle this change?
   —the personnel system
   —the control system

4. If the proposed solution has far-reaching implications, will it be accepted by
   —senior management
   —the public?

Once you've answered these questions, you can confidently propose your solution and its adoption.

SUMMARY

Thoughtful, organized problem solving leads to logical, well-supported arguments. Structured problem solving makes writing reports and memos easier and quicker by:
- Focusing your research
- Generating better solutions
- Giving you a head start on organizing the document
Problem solving is a three-step process:
- Analyze and research the situation
  —draw an analysis tree

—construct a flow chart
—make a need-to-know list
—use primary and secondary sources
—know when to stop
—check for accuracy
● Establish criteria to measure how well alternatives meet objectives
—the writer sets criteria
—criteria are standards
—criteria should be weighted
● Establish and choose among alternatives
—assess alternatives systematically
—write action plans
—test for feasibility

Case Study Exercises

For either **Complex** or **Budget**:

1. Draw an analysis tree for the problem. Drawing the tree is most useful in determining that you have all the parts of the problem and in creating a research framework. In the Budget case, you might draw either of two trees, one using the question, "Is the company likely to pay back the loan?" or one using the question, "On what basis should our bank make this loan?" The analysis tree can also be useful in extracting the advantages and disadvantages of known alternatives. In the Complex Assembly case, you might draw two trees, one dissecting the advantages and disadvantages of sending the faulty wheel assemblies on to High Flying and another showing the advantages and disadvantages of not fulfilling the terms of the original contract.

2. Establish and weight your criteria. Write down the reasons for your choice of criteria and for the weight you gave each one.

3. Judge the alternatives in terms of the criteria, using the form shown in the chapter.

Further References

Flesch, Rudolf. *How to Write, Speak and Think More Effectively.* New York: New American Library, 1951.
Chapters 24–27 contain a lively discussion of creative problem solving. A good, thorough supplement to the system outlined here.

Hodnett, Edward. *The Art of Problem Solving*. New York: Harper & Row, 1955.
For those who want a scholarly treatment of the subject.

Kepner, Charles H. and Tregoe, Benjamin. *The Rational Manager*. New York: McGraw Hill, 1965.
A detailed explanation of the Kepner-Tregoe system of management problem solving.

4
STRUCTURING
YOUR WRITING

Principles you use every day also apply to organizing your writing. This chapter will show you:
- How to group your ideas and information
- How to generalize to draw conclusions
- How to put your information or arguments in logical order
- How to select the order most persuasive for the reader

A mystified executive came to us because he could not understand why top management had refused to adopt his operating plan, the product of months of hard work by the executive and his staff. As we leafed through the hundreds of pages, we began to empathize with the decision makers. There was no summary at the beginning; section followed section in no apparent order; and we found no references in the text to the exhibits. It was easy to see why the plan had been rejected: it was incomprehensible.

The executive and his team had done the research and solved the problem correctly. But when the time came to write it all down, they gave in to the temptation to write selfishly—to march their readers right along with them as they analyzed the issues, sifted through a myriad of alternatives, and finally hit upon some solutions. The path to discovery is often littered with unconnected bits of data and obscured by excursions into unproductive blind alleys. Giving readers the itinerary of such a journey in the form of a disorganized mass of information ultimately gives them nothing.

Once they have finally solved the problem, careful writers always shift their attention back to the reader. They know they must organize the information and arguments so the primary reader will *understand and remember the main points and be persuaded that the writer's position is correct.* Organizing is a two-step process: grouping similar ideas together and ordering the groups logically.

Grouping ideas is essential because the human mind cannot consciously remember more than about seven items or concepts at a time. Several items, or "bits of information," joined together by a common concept, however, become one bit, allowing the mind to organize and label the information. Everyone uses this principle daily: you arrive at the office and begin to plan your day. You know you have to pick up the cleaning and collect the kids on the way home from work. You also have to make a sales call downtown, and you have some banking to do at City National. Scribbling on a scrap of paper, you will probably group your "to do" list geographically, as shown on the next page. Grouping gives you a better chance of remembering that you have two things to do downtown, and you are less likely to leave the kids standing on the curb.

You use the same principle in managing your business affairs. When a production supervisor discovers a similarity in two parts and substitutes one for the other, he is grouping. When a division head places four branches with a common quality under one manager and three branches with a different quality under a second manager, she is grouping.

To do today —
1. In the office
   — Write memo on sales meeting
   — Meet with Tom and Jennifer
2. Downtown
   — Call on Harry Blotz
   — Make deposit in checking
3. On the way home
   — Pick up cleaning
   — Pick up kids

These decision making skills also apply to grouping ideas for writing. Keep this principle in mind as you work through the examples in this chapter: *All ideas of the same kind should be grouped together under a generalization stating what they have in common.*

You also make decisions about ordering every day—when you make up the agenda for a meeting, when you've been out and have to return phone calls, when you decide how to list the names on a transmittal. Unfortunately, many managers who order their work efficiently do not think to use the same process when they sit down to prepare a report or memo. Readers depend on writers to present information and arguments in a rational order. Once you've grouped your ideas, you'll need to decide on a sensible way to order them, based on the purpose of the memo or report and the reader's likely reaction to it.

Grouping and Ordering for Description

Grouping and ordering are important even when the communi-cation is descriptive. One major equipment-leasing company, for example, provides stock paragraphs to use in letters confirming sales or lease agreements. These paragraphs have the following headings:

```
Opening
Customer's Responsibilities
Leasing Plans
Available Training Programs
Features of the X-2900 Duplicator
Maintenance Obligations
Service Options
Mammoth Equipment's Responsibilities
Warranties
```

The Opening thanks the customers for ordering an X-2900 duplicator. (The company encourages the sales representatives to fill in the details of their conversations with purchasers in the remainder of the paragraph.) The stock paragraphs are provided in the order given above, and the sales representatives usually plug them in to the letter as given. Disregarding for the moment that an effective letter needs transitions to orient the reader, look at the paragraph headings. Are you asking why the writer chose to put Customer's Responsibilities first and Leasing Plans second? Are you trying to figure out what the connection is? There's a good reason for your confusion. The mind naturally assumes that things that are presented together go together *in some sense*. If the relationship is not immediately apparent, the mind will expend a fair amount of energy trying to figure out the connection before giving up in frustration. By following the rule of grouping, you may be able to find relationships that the Mammoth Equipment sales department ignored.

First, try to find ideas that belong together. Picture the heading of each section of the Mammoth Equipment letter written on a three-by-five-inch card. Can you shuffle the cards around to form logical groups? Perhaps your eye is caught by the fact that "Responsibilities" is mentioned twice. Since this is a letter confirming a contractual agreement, it is likely that the nature of the responsibilities is the most important concept. You would take the two three-by-five-inch cards on which Customer's Responsibilities and Mammoth Equipment's Responsibilities are written and separate them out as major subdivisions of the letter:

```
┌─────────────────────────┐   ┌─────────────────────────┐
│                         │   │                         │
│       Customer's        │   │   Mammoth Equipment's   │
│     Responsibilities    │   │     Responsibilities    │
│                         │   │                         │
│                         │   │                         │
└─────────────────────────┘   └─────────────────────────┘
```

Now look at the rest of the headings. Do any of them refer to responsibilities of any kind? The section on Warranties probably fits in this category—no doubt it contains a description of Mammoth Equipment's legal obligations—as does the section on Maintenance Obligations. So you slip those cards under the Mammoth Equipment's Responsibilities card, where their position will remind you that they are subsections.

Looking at the other headings, you notice that all but one of them seem to describe not responsibilities but options or choices available to the customer. They are Leasing Plans, Available Training Programs, and Service Options. Conceivably, these could all be grouped together as subsections of a heading that does not yet exist, that is, Customer Options. This title immediately tells the reader just how the three subsections relate to each other—they are all options. To complete the exercise, you write Customer Options on a card and place the others beneath it.

One heading, or unit, remains in the original list of sections: Features of the X-2900 Duplicator. Does it relate to anything else? If the paragraph merely describes the machine, it may be only introductory material. If it describes those functions of the machine that require specially trained operators, however, it may be a subsection of the Training Programs section.

The point is that, even in a relatively straightforward document, grouping sections or ideas and making generalizations about each group will get your point across most efficiently and clearly. Consider the reorganization of the letter shown on page 50.

This simple example illustrates how writers use grouping and ordering to refine their thinking and to focus on the needs of the reader. In this case, regrouping led to reordering. Only a few quick decisions were needed to determine the most logical order and the most palatable presentation for customers. For a document

```
Opening Paragraph
```

Features of the X-2900 Duplicator [*You've decided
that this section merely describes the features of the machine and is
intended only to refresh the reader's memory. Therefore you've put it
in as introduction.*]

Mammoth Equipment's Responsibilities [*You've decided
that responsibilities are more important than options and so should
go first. You've also decided that it is politic to tell the customers
what you are obligated to do for them before telling them what they
are required to do for you.*]

```
    Warranties

    Maintenance Obligations

Customer's Responsibilities

Customer's Options

    Leasing plans

    Training programs

    Service options
```

that will describe or inform, choosing an appropriate order is usually simple. You have several options:

1. **Hierarchical**—you are describing an organizational chart, so you go from the highest position to the lowest.

2. **Geographical**—you are describing a company's operations in various regions throughout the country, so you might proceed from east to west.

3. **Chronological**—you are presenting a history of a trade book publishing in the Midwest, so you start with the founding of the first regional trade book firm and work your way up to the present.

4. **Steps in a Process**—you are telling the reader about the new assembly line procedures, so you consider the first step first and the other steps in sequence.

5. **Most Important to Least Important**—you're discussing product lines, so you begin with the most profitable and end with the least. Remember that, unlike the first four orders, the order here is clearly a matter of judgment. You should take special care to make sure that your reader will agree that your assessment of the importance of the components is reasonable.

Of course, you may decide to use one order for the body of the report and others where appropriate for subsections of the same document.

Take a descriptive memo you wrote recently and jot down the major ideas in the order in which they are discussed. Are the points grouped logically? Do you make a generalization about each grouping? Have they been presented in a rational order that meets the reader's needs?

Organizing Criteria and Alternatives for Evaluation

The Mammoth Equipment grouping and ordering exercise was fairly easy because the paragraphs are largely descriptive. When you are developing criteria and evaluating alternatives, organizing is a bit more complicated. If you have more than a few criteria, you should consider grouping them. No reader can mentally juggle three alternatives and ten criteria and at the same time keep track of the comparisons.

Grouping may help eliminate extraneous criteria that at first seem important. A staff member of a hospital cost commission, for instance, grouped his criteria for evaluating three hospitals that had applied for a CAT scanner, a sophisticated machine for detecting tumors. Only one application could be accepted. Test your judgment against the staff member's grouping. He began with a rather long list:

```
The hospital to be approved must:

1. Be the hospital most centrally located.
2. Be able to finance the machine at the most ad-
   vantageous interest rates.
3. Serve the greatest number of indigent patients.
4. Be accessible to the largest number of aged
   patients.
5. Have facilities that can be most easily adapted
   to accommodate the machine.
6. Be the hospital to which the region's doctors
   prefer to admit patients.
7. Have an administration that is able to deal
   with the complexities of scheduling use of the
   machine for an entire region.
8. Demonstrate that it has a technical staff that
   can deal with the machine.
9. Be able to absorb the cost of financing the ma-
   chine in its operating budget.
```

The staff member read over his list to make sure all the criteria were standards against which the hospitals could be judged. He eliminated criterion 7 (have an administration that is able to deal with the complexities of scheduling use of the machine for an entire region) on the grounds that it was not measurable. All the other criteria, he felt, were standards against which the commission could judge the hospitals.

Could any of the criteria be grouped? The staff member noted that numbers 1, 3, and 4 all dealt with patient care. However, he decided they were potentially in conflict because serving the greatest number of indigent and aged patients was not necessarily consistent with central location. He decided that central geographic location was a meaningless criterion, because sufficient and various transportation routes existed in the area. He also noted that poverty-stricken and aged patients required CAT scans no more frequently than any other patients. He then formulated the following, more general, criterion:

1. The hospital should be accessible to the largest patient population.

Next he looked over the remaining criteria and grouped numbers 2 (ability to finance the machine at the most advantageous interest rates) and 9 (capacity to absorb the cost of financing the machine in its operating budget). Both related to the capacity of a hospital to finance the purchase of the machine. The staff member felt this was the major point to consider and that details about whether the hospital ultimately leased the machine and at what rate, or whether it financed the machine and at what rate, were immaterial. He created this criterion:

2. The hospital should show the lowest costs for acquiring, installing, and using the CAT scanner.

Although he had initially felt that numbers 5 (adaptable facilities) and 8 (technical staff) might be part of a criterion based on technology, he decided that possession of facilities that can be most easily adapted to accommodate the machine could be offset by allocation of funds for renovation. Whether the hospital had technicians who could run the machine or whether it would have to hire them was also a question of cost. As a result, the staff member resolved to consider these issues when he weighed the alternatives against his new criterion 2.

Criterion 6, which dealt with the preferences of doctors for one hospital, was now the only original criterion left, and the staff member eliminated this on the grounds that doctors would go where the machine was located.

Through grouping, he had arrived at two major criteria against which to judge alternatives:

1. The hospital should be accessible to the greatest number of patients.
2. The hospital should show the lowest costs for acquiring, installing, and using the CAT scanner.

Other ways can be found to group these nine criteria. The point is to limit the criteria to those that are meaningful to the readers—

in this instance, a hospital cost commission concerned with patient care and expenses.

The staff member is now ready to group and order his arguments according to criteria or alternatives. In general, it is more effective to consider how each alternative meets each criterion than to consider all the pros and cons of an alternative before going on to the next alternative. When you group and order around criteria, comparisons among alternatives are easy to make. If the staff member knows that costs are uppermost in the minds of the commissioners and that they will accept his criteria as valid, he may decide simply to discuss the three hospitals first in terms of costs and then in terms of patient care. If, however, he feels his readers need to be persuaded that his two criteria are sufficient for judging the alternatives, he'll spend some time justifying the criteria before using them to assess the hospitals. If he thinks the commission is biased in favor of a hospital that does not meet the criteria, he will need to make a strong case for the validity of the criteria, taking care to anticipate the readers' biases so that he can later demonstrate that the favored hospital doesn't measure up. He will then have to decide whether to dispose of the popular but unworkable alternative before or after examining the other two hospitals in the light of the criteria. Whichever order he chooses, he must weigh the alternatives and allow the commission to draw the safest and soundest conclusion. That, after all, is his job. The order in which a writer presents criteria and alternatives, along with the position or emphasis he assigns them, derives not only from logic, but also from the reader's needs and expectations.

Organizing for a Recommendation

When you make a recommendation, you are arguing for your point of view. Arguments in support of a point lose their impact if they are not kept together and presented logically. Furthermore, the reader may not make the right connections if forced to gather supporting evidence from different parts of the document.

You must be able to convince the reader that you have correctly solved the problem and then persuade the reader to act on your recommendation. If you and the reader agree on the definition of the problem, you may be able to justify your conclusions with a few statements in the introduction:

Your department has been under attack for not staying within bud-getary limits. You must now set goals and define ways to meet them that will reestablish your credibility with the senior staff.

This statement of the problem will be sufficient if you and the reader agree that the reader's loss of credibility results from over-spending. If the reader suspects his image has been tarnished for some other reason, you will have to group and order evidence in support of your definition of the problem before suggesting solu-tions.

Grouping Evidence and Arguments

For a simple argument, jotting down your main ideas and grouping them informally may be enough. For complex arguments requiring extensive support, however, it's helpful to group on pa-per. Sorting your supporting evidence into manageable packages and making appropriate generalizations gives you a start on check-ing the logic of your conclusion. Writing it down gives you a visual check on your argument and lets you see whether you've grouped to the highest meaningful level of generalization. To do this, it is convenient to use a form like this one:

Grouping Form

Findings	Generalizations	Further Generalizations
_____		
_____	_____	
_____		
		_____
_____		
_____	_____	
_____		
		_____
_____		
_____	_____	
_____		

By listing like assertions together on the left and the generalization about them to their right, you can see if there are further generalizations you can make.

The president of a small chain of successful department stores was concerned that the proliferation of boutiques in his geographic area might ultimately cut into his business. His most profitable line was higher-priced junior clothing, and he wondered if he could compete with the new boutiques by opening smaller stores carrying only the junior line. He had two locations in mind, one in a rapidly expanding office complex in a major city and the other in a suburban shopping center. He turned to his most experienced store manager for help in evaluating the idea. If the manager believed the idea was sound, she was to assess both locations in terms of potential profitability and recommend one.

After analyzing the situation, the manager agreed that opening a boutique was a worthwhile experiment. She looked at both locations and decided that the potential for profits was greater in the city, listing the following reasons:

```
Working women need more clothes and accessories
than homemakers.

Working women have more money to spend on clothes
than homemakers.

Working women have less time to shop than
homemakers and are more likely to choose the store
they shop in based on convenience.

Many suburban families are moving back into the
city because of gas shortages.

Five thousand women between twenty and forty work
in the downtown office complex area.

A building with offices employing 2,000 workers is
planned for a site three blocks away from the
existing office complex.

The downtown office complex is located near bus and
subway terminals.
```

> There is no department store within ten blocks of
> the complex.
>
> There are only three shops in the downtown area
> that merchandise women's wear.
>
> Studies show working women shop in stores that
> cater to them.
>
> Men buy gifts for women on impulse.

After a couple of false starts, some rethinking, and the elimination or addition of one or two assertions, the manager came up with the grouping shown in figure 4.1.

Setting groupings out in this way allowed the writer to see whether the generalizations really supported the argument she had decided to make and whether the groupings were the most useful for supporting that argument. You might, in this case, generalize further that the mall has a large population of potential shoppers, some of whom already work there and some of whom can be induced to come to the area to shop. As a result, you would be left with only two major assertions.

If you want to test your grouping skills further, turn to Appendix 3 and see if you agree with the way the consultant to the candy manufacturer grouped the ideas she intended to mention in her report.

For the next memo you write, consider what action you want the reader to take. Jot down all your important ideas and use the Grouping Form to group them to support your main assertion before you write the memo.

Ordering a Memo or Report that Recommends

In choosing the order for a report or memo that includes a recommendation, you will need to determine the sequence that will be most understandable and convincing to your primary reader. You should make this decision based on your authority to propose action and your reader's probable reaction to your proposal.

Figure 4.1
Grouping Evidence and Arguments

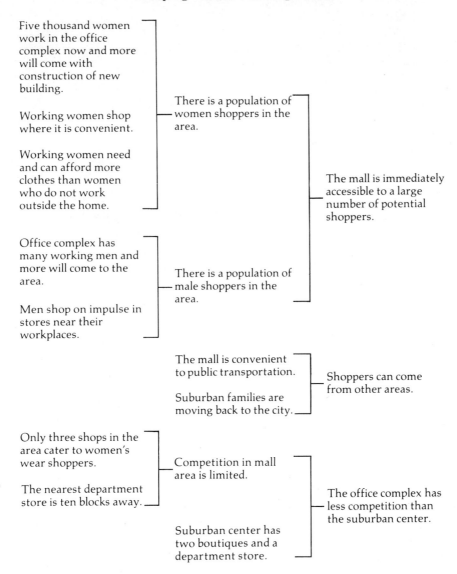

Recommendations first or last? The most important decision you make regarding the order of a report or memo is whether to put your recommendations first or last. We strongly suggest that *your memo or report will be most effective if you put your recommendations first.* If you have a forceful argument, using the "recommendations-first" method allows the reader to instantly grasp what you're saying and lays the groundwork for an understanding of your supporting points.

Some managers believe that you should save recommendations for last, on the theory that it is more persuasive to present first all the evidence and reasons for a recommendation or conclusion. Although a reader may indeed marvel at your thoroughness and flashes of insight as you proceed from gathering data to drawing conclusions, you can't rely on that. In fact, the reader may refuse to play the game of mutual discovery with you at all. After spending the first several minutes (many psychologists believe this is the most valuable learning time) trying to figure out where you are headed, the reader may simply give up. Or, if you are lucky, a veteran in dealing with writers who use this method may flip to the end to find out what you are really proposing. If you can honestly say that you believe knowing the substance of the recommendation will prejudice the reader's acceptance of your arguments, leave it for last. More often than not, though, writers are reluctant to start with their recommendations because they are unwilling to take a stand. This attitude may be left over from academic days, when the logic of the argument got more points than the answer and a decision might be avoided altogether—a situation that does not exist in the management world.

Ordering the supporting arguments. Now that your recommendation is in place, you will begin to order the body of your report or memo. A **deductive** order is based on a deductive argument; it requires you to work according to a strict plan, stating and supporting interlocking premises that lead to a logical conclusion. If you do adopt such a design, in which each step leads to the next and succeeding statements depend on the validity of preceding statements, you should be aware that you may spend most of your time proving your major and minor premises to convince the reader that your conclusion is valid. The department store manager who wants to convince the president to open a downtown boutique might decide to structure her argument this way:

| Working women shop in boutiques that are accessible. | → | The downtown office complex is accessible to working women. | ∴ | A boutique downtown will attract working women shoppers. |

Since the combination of assertions dictates the order of the argument, she will have no choice but to unlock the answer step by step, beginning with the first premise, proving it, and proceeding to the next. If she proves that both premises are true, her conclusion, "A boutique downtown will attract working women shoppers," must therefore be valid, and the reader will be forced to agree. Since most of us solve problems deductively, it is easy to fall back on this approach to explain a conclusion. The manager will make her point. But, because deductive arguments tend to be repetitious, her choice of structure may require an excessive expenditure of time and energy for both writer and reader.

Although deductive arguments are unimaginative, they come in handy for building airtight cases or persuading recalcitrant readers, some of whom may need to be trapped by logic. Some arguments lend themselves to this structure; complicated presentations usually require a form that is less restrictive and more creative. Furthermore, unless you have the deductive powers of a Sherlock Holmes or a Perry Mason, you would do well not to risk being locked in by your own formula.

A document based on an **inductive** order—in which the main statement is supported by a collection of assertions and data—is grounded in an inductive argument. Such memos and reports are more interesting to read than deductively ordered documents because the conclusion is based on a leap of faith—it is not dictated by the logic of the argument. The reader is invited to participate in your thinking and can feel free to judge the accuracy of your conclusion independently. A government economist might structure an argument this way:

Main statement: Auto City, Michigan, is already suffering from the recession.
Support: —Capitol Airlines has abandoned its Cleveland–Auto City route.
—Unemployment stands at 12.5 percent.
—Sales in area stores are 35 percent below last year's sales.

In this kind of argument, the parts *add* up to the whole—not *lead* up to the whole, as they do in a deductive argument.

Each piece of writing presents a unique challenge because it requires you to find an order that works best for the memo or report as a whole, for each section, and for the reader. Moreover, you, the writer, must feel comfortable with the design you choose. If you are by nature straightforward, all your good attempts to introduce elliptical arguments for the sake of variety may result in nothing but frustration or, worse yet, an unduly elaborate structure. How, then, should you go about striking a delicate balance among all these considerations and still come up with a writing design that will work?

You have accumulated all your facts and evidence, and by now you have inferred your conclusion based on your best assessment of the data, which may include both statistical evidence and the past experience of experts in your field. If you have faith in your recommendation, you will organize to support your conviction. If you have "read" your reader, you will arrange your writing in an order that will be convincing, interesting, and accessible. Here are some possible orders:

1. Most important to least important. The executives we talked to expressed a strong preference for this order, for one obvious reason: it is easy to read. You should use it whenever you have a solid argument and an objective reader. You can then place less important or negative evidence in subsections or minor positions. Busy and distracted managers may not read your entire document. Using this order insures that they will be likely to read your most convincing arguments.

2. Least controversial to most controversial. Psychologists' studies indicate that readers are more likely to accept an author's argument if they agree with the first thing they read. Giving the most obvious, or least objectionable, information first may enlist the reader's support for the rest of the report or memo. If the reader agrees with the first argument you offer in support of your conclusion, you will have established credibility, increasing the likelihood that the rest of your assertions will be viewed positively.

3. Negative to positive. Whether you are writing to compare alternatives or to recommend, objectivity demands that you mention the less favorable points as well as the more favorable. If the reader is already aware of the negative implication or needs to be impressed by your objectivity, it is most persuasive to place the cons ahead of the pros:

> Although construction costs in Denver are slightly higher than they are in Farmington and Houston, these costs will be offset in the long run by tax credits.

In this case readers will encounter your positive argument last, where it is in a position of strength.

Look at a recent memo that dealt with a controversial topic. What kind of order did you use? Recommendation first or last? Do you feel you chose the most persuasive order?

SUMMARY

Your writing will have a much better chance of being understood and accepted if you organize your ideas and information, keeping the following points in mind:
- For descriptive documents, place all ideas of the same kind together and formulate a generalization covering the commonality of each group
- Descriptive reports may be ordered in these possible forms:
  —hierarchical
  —geographical
  —chronological
  —enumeration of steps
  —most important to least important
- For reports or memos that evaluate, all criteria of the same kind should be grouped together and restated, if possible, as a broader criterion
- Depending on the reader's needs, the report may then be ordered according to
  —criteria
  —alternatives
- For a document that argues for a recommendation
  —all findings in support of the same conclusion should be placed together under a generalization
  —all conclusions in support of the same recommendation should be placed together under an appropriate generalization
- To find a design that best supports your recommendation, you should decide
  —whether to put recommendations first or last
  —whether to use a deductive or an inductive argument for the whole or parts of your document
- To find a design that suits both your recommendation and your readers, you should consider these options:
  —most important to least important
  —least controversial to most controversial
  —negative to positive

Case Study Exercises

1. **Complex.** Assume you are Russo writing to Senior Management. (a) Group your ideas in support of your recommendation. (b) Consider two possible orders for presenting your arguments and jot down your ideas regarding each, stating what effect you think each will have on the readers, the logic of the presentation, and your credibility as the writer. (c) Consider how Russo would group and order his argument in a memo to Pilawski.

2. **Budget.** Assume you are Lerue writing to the investment committee. (a) Group the criteria for your decision; (b) then group your ideas in support of your recommendation. (c) Decide whether your recommendation should go first or last; (d) decide whether you should discuss criteria before supporting your recommendation. Jot down your reasons for your decisions.

Further References

Beardsley, Monroe C. *Writing with Reason.* Englewood Cliffs, NJ: Prentice-Hall, 1976.
An exhaustive but pragmatic discussion of all forms of argument, geared to the needs of writers.

Fogelin, Robert J. *Understanding Arguments: An Introduction to Informal Logic.* New York: Harcourt Brace Jovanovich, 1978.
Provides an extensive discussion of all forms of arguments. For those who want to analyze their own skills more closely.

Gallagher, William J. *Report Writing for Management.* Reading, MA: Addison-Wesley, 1969.
Beginning on page 46, Gallagher gives a good short explanation of induction and deduction. This book also provides a good in-depth discussion of the specifics of report writing.

Karlins, Marvin, and Abelson, Herbert. *Persuasion.* New York: Springer, 1970.
Short summaries of psychological studies of persuasion. Valuable discussion of choosing a persuasive order.

Van Nostrand, A. D., et al. *Functional Writing.* Boston: Houghton Mifflin Co., 1977.
This book contains a nice section on grouping ideas.

Walter, Otis M. and Scott, Robert L. *Thinking and Speaking.* London: Macmillan, 1968.
   Although aimed at preparing speakers, the principles in chapter 5 apply to writers as well.

5

PICTURING
YOUR STRATEGY

Drawing a picture of your report or memo is probably the most crucial and beneficial step you will take before actually writing a draft. This chapter will show you:

- How to choose the right diagram for your purpose
- How to use an organization tree or pyramid to check the logic of your argument
- How to improve your use of the old-fashioned linear outline
- How to develop storyboards that incorporate your illustrations and transitions

Once you've grouped your ideas and decided on their most logical
order, you should picture your argument on paper, checking its
validity and formalizing your generalizations by making them into
complete sentences. Diagramming the argument actually helps
you write many parts of the memo or report and establish its final
form. If the picture is well done, writing the first draft will go
quickly because you will simply be connecting well-thought-out
and carefully worded ideas. The sections of the diagram will be
the sections of the final document, and the headings will come
directly from the picture.

For any report written by more than one person, drawing a picture of the final argument insures that everyone involved agrees
on what will be included and eliminates the chance for redundancies, oversights ("I thought you were going to cover that point"),
or misunderstandings ("But I thought we were going to compare
financial data, not talk about management systems").

Different Pictures for Different Purposes

You can draw a picture of your argument in one of four ways: as
an organization tree, a pyramid, a linear outline, or a storyboard.
Organization trees and pyramids, which highlight the relationships among assertions, are indispensable tools for testing your
logic and are natural extensions of the problem solving methods.
you've been using. They help you organize the body of your report. (Beginnings and endings follow different rules and are discussed in chapter 6.) The traditional, linear outline comes naturally
to some writers; however, it is less useful than a pyramid or organization tree because it does not emphasize relationships. The
storyboard, as the name implies, provides a story line—it forces
you to develop thesis statements and transitions and indicates
where visuals are needed.

Whatever kind of picture you choose, you should write your
main assertions as full sentences. This procedure makes you pay
attention to the wording of your argument, encourages you to
define your terms and support each portion of your argument,
and provides you with polished sentences to include in the first
draft.

Drawing an Organization Tree

The organization tree is an extension of the analysis tree you
used in chapter 3 to solve the problem. You may remember that
for simple descriptions you can frequently use the analysis tree as

the framework for your first draft, checking only to be certain you have included all the parts of the whole, and that your assertions support the point to the left of them and are parallel in thought and structure.

For recommendation memos or reports, you'll draw a new tree, writing your conclusion, recommendation, or summary statement on the single line on the left and developing supporting evidence on the branches (see figure 5.1). If you are comparing three alternative locations and grouping and ordering your argument around criteria, the tree you would draw might look like the one the writer drew in figure 5.2. The criteria and the assertions about each location came directly from the problem solving work described in chapter 3.

To check the organization tree for flaws in logical development, you should look at each row on the tree. Do all assertions connected by lines to the generalization immediately to their left relate to that assertion in the same way? That is, are they parallel in con-

Figure 5.1
Organization Tree Using Reasons

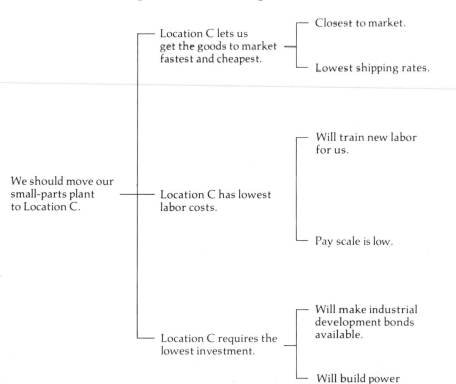

cept? For example, in figure 5.1, "Location C will allow us to get the goods to market," "Location C has the lowest labor costs," and "Location C requires the lowest investment" are all *reasons* to move the small parts plant to Location C. In figure 5.2, the row of assertions immediately to the right of the summary statement are all *criteria*. All the assertions to the right of the criteria are statements about *how the alternatives meet the criteria*.

It is not necessary that all statements in each row be of the same kind, but it is necessary that all statements supporting one assertion be of the same type, i.e., reasons, steps, parts of a whole, or alternatives. In figure 5.3, the recommendation is supported by two reasons. One of these is supported by more reasons and the other by steps telling how to make a profitable substitute.

Figure 5.2
Organization Tree Using Criteria

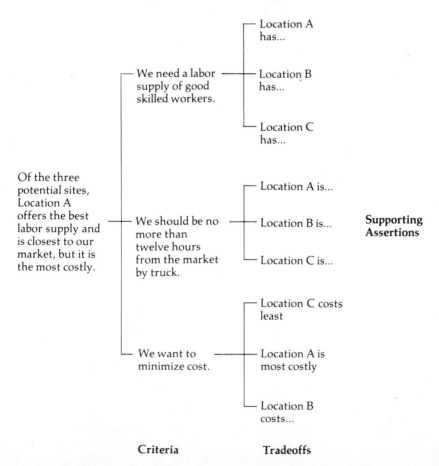

Figure 5.3
Organization Tree Using Reasons and Steps

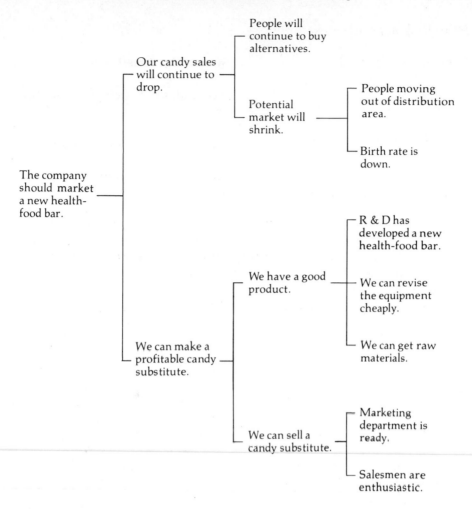

As you check the tree, be certain that all the supporting assertions for an inductive argument provide proof of the general assertion:

General Assertion   **Supporting Assertions**

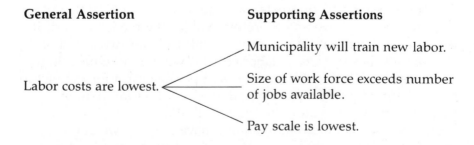

These assertions all give reasons for low labor costs.

Now look at another example:

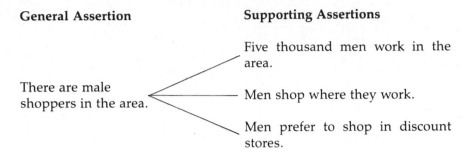

General Assertion

There are male shoppers in the area.

Supporting Assertions

Five thousand men work in the area.

Men shop where they work.

Men prefer to shop in discount stores.

The statement, "Men prefer to shop in discount stores," may be true, but it does not support the assertion that "there are male shoppers in the area."

All points supporting an assertion should also be parallel in form:

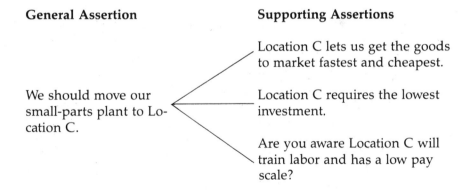

General Assertion

We should move our small-parts plant to Location C.

Supporting Assertions

Location C lets us get the goods to market fastest and cheapest.

Location C requires the lowest investment.

Are you aware Location C will train labor and has a low pay scale?

The third assertion, formulated as a question, is not parallel in form to the other two and therefore will jar the reader's mind. If it is cast as a statement, in conformity with the first two assertions, "Location C has the lowest labor cost," it will be more meaningful to the reader. Writing full sentences in parallel form for the picture of your argument will guarantee that you will write them in parallel form when you write the first draft.

Finally, each generalization should have at least two subdivisions; every deductive argument must be based on at least two premises, and every inductive argument must be based on a generalization from at least two pieces of evidence. This is easy to see on the organization tree. If you find you have only one subdivision, check to see if you have dropped off a premise or failed to give enough evidence.

Using a Pyramid Diagram

The pyramid diagram, developed in detail by writing consultant Barbara Minto, provides a visual interpretation of a deductive or an inductive argument. Like the organization tree, the pyramid does not include the introduction of your report or memo, but pictures the argument and its supporting evidence.

In a deductive argument, as shown in figure 5.4, the topmost box represents the main point. The boxes underneath show the syllogism, or series of dependent premises, you are using as evidence. According to convention, the major premise is always placed on the far left. As you can see, each of the premises must be supported by evidence, which may be developed inductively or deductively. The pyramid provides a good visual representation of a deductive argument because the major and minor premises appear next to each other on a horizontal line and their relationship (or lack of it) is easy to see.

The pyramid can also be used effectively to picture an inductive argument. In figure 5.5, both assertions at the level below the top box relate to the recommendation in the same way—they are both reasons. Each of these reasons is supported by another set of reasons. The next level of assertions in a memo or short report will usually be supporting data. However, it is not necessary for all arguments to go to the same level of detail.

As you can see, the only difference between the organization tree and the pyramid is that one moves from left to right and the other from the top down. Although both forms are equally useful for picturing an inductive argument, the logic of a deductive argument is more easily followed on a pyramid.

Choose something you have written recently (rule of thumb—not so recently that you are still thoroughly sick of it, but not so long ago you no longer care about it) and draw a picture of it, using either the organization tree or the pyramid. Now ask yourself these questions:

- *Did diagramming the paper bring to light any need for improvement?*

Figure 5.4
Pyramid Diagram Showing a Deductive Argument

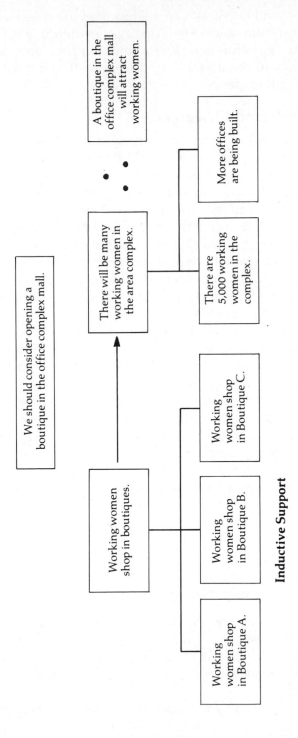

Figure 5.5
Pyramid Diagram Showing an Inductive Argument

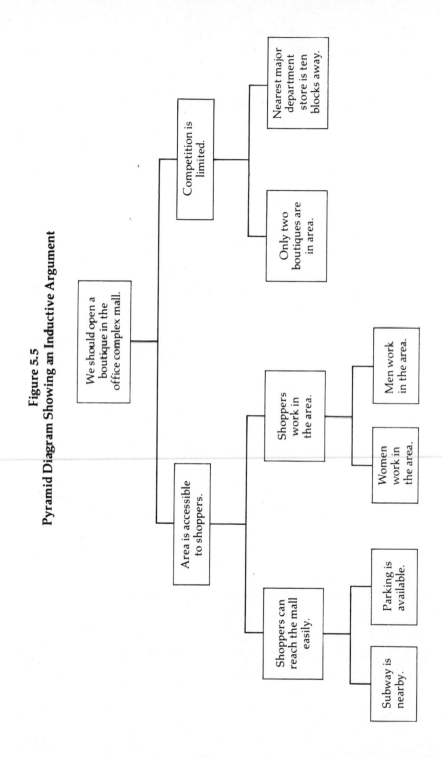

- *Could a reader easily follow the argument?*
- *Are there any sections that "don't fit" or appear unrelated to the train of thought?*
- *Are there any places an argument or assertion isn't supported?*

Now take a few minutes and rearrange the elements of your diagram to make it more effective. In your next writing assignment, diagram your argument before you write.

Using the Linear Outline

Everyone knows what this outline looks like—it's the one your fifth grade teacher made you use to outline the social studies text, possibly the best exercise ever devised for developing a healthy skepticism of scholarly views. Its connection with past unpleasantries has made some writers resist it. However, if you're accustomed to using it, it can help you organize your ideas. A good linear outline also can be converted, almost unchanged, into the contents page for a long report.

Suppose you want to suggest that your company hire a freelance professional to develop the annual report this year. You use the introduction to bring your reader up to the point of departure, perhaps by explaining that last year's annual report was a fiasco. That introduction will be Roman numeral I (one). Now you want to make sure your main line of reasoning is valid. So you outline. You pick up your major points, arrived at by grouping, and make them Roman numerals II, III, IV, putting them in the order you worked out:

```
  I.  Introduction

 II.  A professional can insure the production of
      an accurate and complete report.

III.  A professional can help the corporation use
      graphic design and new printing techniques to
      the best advantage.

 IV.  A professional will produce a less costly
      report than we can create in-house.
```

Your next task is to group your evidence so that you provide sufficient proof for each of your assertions. The strongest form of proof is another assertion, backed by supporting evidence. Therefore, the ideal formal outline of a document that seeks to convince looks like this:

Linear Outline Format

I. Major Assertion
    A. Minor assertion
       1. Evidence 1
       2. Evidence 2
    B. Minor assertion
II. Major Assertion
    (and so on).

An expanded version of the outline supporting hiring a professional might look like this:

```
  I. A professional can insure the production of
     an accurate and complete report.
     A.  An outsider can ignore inappropriate
         attempts to influence the report's
         content.
         1. Departments are competing for coverage
            in the report.
         2. Departments have a natural tendency to
            bury the bad news.
     B.  We do not have adequate staff to check
         details and data.

 II. A professional can help the corporation use
     new printing and graphic design techniques to
     the best advantage.
     A.  We are not equipped to choose among the
         many new types of reproduction.
```

```
            1. We do not know what is available.
            2. We do not have the expertise to select
               the most attractive graphics.
         B. Extensive use of photography and graphics
            in reports requires design skills we do
            not have in-house.

   III. A professional will produce the report more
        efficiently than we can.
        A. He or she will take less time.
        B. He or she will prevent us from making
           costly mistakes.
```

By writing full sentences you will avoid confusing *description* with *evidence*. If you think, "New types of reproduction," ask yourself, *"What about* new types of reproduction? New types of reproduction will . . ."* If it doesn't support your argument, scrap it.

The same rules that apply to using an organization tree or pyramid also apply to using a linear outline. All points supporting a major assertion should be parallel in concept (relate to that assertion in the same way) and parallel in structure. Linear outlines, however, do not force you to write down the thesis statement. Furthermore, because the major assertions are separated by supporting assertions and evidence, it is difficult to check the logic of the argument, and you may miss major flaws in relationships and structure. We suggest, therefore, that you use the linear outline only to develop the internal sections of a long report. If you have a strong personal preference for it, at least check the major points supporting your conclusion by using the organization tree or pyramid.

Working with the Storyboard

If the supporting evidence for your argument is largely statistical, consider using a storyboard, which encourages you to take your visuals into account. A storyboard consists of a number of segments—one for each section of the report. By spreading the storyboard out in front of you, you can see the sequence of the report and can move sections around before you begin to write. You begin each segment of the storyboard by writing a major assertion in the box headed "thesis statement." For example, look at figure 5.6, a segment of a storyboard used by the staff of the Industrial Planning Commission of Frost County to organize a report on the options available to the county to expand its tax base. This segment of the storyboard outlines a proposal to encourage light industry to move to East River. The thesis statement is "Frost County can double light industrial production in the East River section." The support for that assertion—that appropriate sites exist, that facilities are attractive, and that trained workers are available—is backed up by maps and a table. The transition sentence, "Companies interested in locating in the valley adjoining the East River section would provide a market for East River light industry," appears at the bottom, and leads to the next segment of the storyboard, "Several companies are interested in locating in the

Figure 5.6
Storyboard

Thesis Statement:

Frost County can double light industrial production in the East River section.

Supporting Statements:	Data: Charts, Tables
Sites are available for two new industrial parks.	Map showing existing and proposed sites.
Facilities are attractive to light industry.	Map
—good highway access —adequate electrical power	
The community college provides trained workers.	Table showing enrollment and training.

Transition Sentence:

Companies interested in locating in the adjoining valley would provide a market for East River light industry.

valley." (In using the storyboard, the first level of support should always be written out in full sentences; in a short report the secondary support may be abbreviated.)

Using a storyboard forces you (1) to produce topic sentences, (2) to cast transition sentences, and (3) to justify your inclusion of a particular chart or table. In addition, it provides a usable outline for an oral presentation. However, unlike the organization tree and the pyramid, the storyboard does not let you "see" the relationships among the various parts of your argument. You can partially compensate for this deficiency by carefully wording your transition statements. Phrases such as "furthermore" or "in addition" signal that your next point is similar in kind to the one that preceded it, and "as a result," "therefore," and "consequently" tell you either that one thing caused another or that you are drawing an inference based on the preceding point. Although transitions help to provide valuable signs of direction, the storyboard is best used to develop sections of a long report for which the major arguments are shown on an organization tree or pyramid.

You can check your organizational skills now by looking at this formal outline and the organization tree in figure 5.7. They are based on the Budget Finance case study. Can you see flaws in the outline?

```
I. Budget Finance is a small, well-managed
   company.
   A.  The management team has broad experience
       1. In finance
       2. In administration
       3. In sales.
   B.  Mr. Ephram is an able salesman with charm.
   C.  Ephram's partner has accounting and bank
       experience.
   D.  Ephram's partner has links to the Spanish-
       speaking community.
   E.  The company has trained personnel to deal
       with people.
```

II. Budget can counter the causes of high default
    rates.
    A. Budget purchases all contracts from
        retailers it does business with.
    B. Budget gets a 20 percent down payment.
    C. Budget keeps reserves until it gets full
        payment.
    D. Budget provides management advice to
        retailers.
    E. Budget provides customers with special
        services.
        1. It uses bilingual communications.
        2. It serves as intermediary in retailer-
           customer disagreements.

III. Budget is an efficiently run organization.
    A. Company is fully computerized.
    B. Company acts like a big company.
        1. Budget uses large law firm.
        2. Budget publishes audited financial
           statements.
        3. Budget uses extensive personnel
           training.

 IV. Budget maintains reserves to protect itself
    in case of losses.
    A. Company keeps reserves.
    B. Retailer has vested interest in keeping
        customer happy.

  V. Earnings will quadruple by 1974.

 VI. Financing Budget fits our community policy.

VII. Budget's business should grow, based on
     national data.

Figure 5.7
Organization Tree Showing Relationships

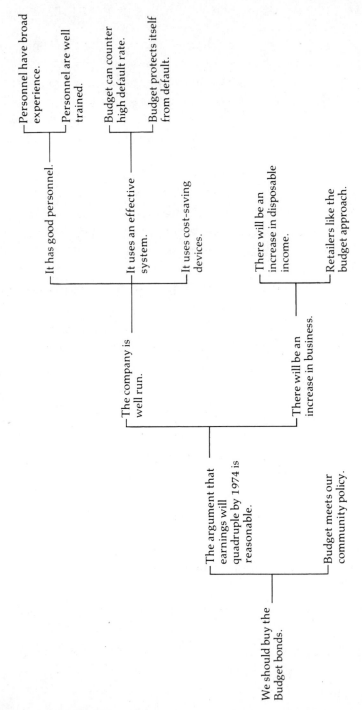

This outline has many problems—here are a few:

- Management's connection to the Spanish-speaking community is not a function of being well managed.
- Acting like a big company does not indicate efficiency.
- Although countering high default rates and protecting against them are two different concepts, they are sufficiently similar that they should not be separated by another topic.
- Seven major assertions are probably too many for a short memo. Some of the major assertions should be grouped. The difference between "well-managed" and "efficiently run" is narrow. These major assertions should be combined.

Another way to approach these data would be to draw an organization tree that more clearly shows relationships (see figure 5.7). It should be clear from the tree that the writer of this report needs evidence to support the assertion that Budget meets the bank's community policy. As you can see, some of the assertions and reasons on the linear outline support such points as good personnel (qualities of individuals, training) and good approaches (limit default rate, cover potential losses from the remaining default rate). The argument set out on the organization tree is tight and the number of major assertions is limited.

Checking your Strategy

Regardless of the kind of diagram or outline you use, it is wise to review it before you begin to write. This is an opportunity to look at your argument as a whole and to check its logic and validity. The following checklist is a good guide:

Diagramming Checklist

1. Does the thesis sentence state your major point and nothing else?

2. Does each generalization include all the supporting statements and nothing else?

3. Are all the generalizations supported by at least two subpoints?

4. Are statements written in full declarative sentences (no questions, no phrases)?

5. For inductively ordered support—
     Do all points in support of a generalization relate to the generalization in the same way? (Are they all reasons, or steps, or parts of a whole?)

6. For deductively ordered support—
     Are the premises truly dependent? Do they lead unequivocally to your conclusion?

7. For both—
     Does the support for each generalization or assertion answer every question the reader might ask?

8. Did you consider the reader's needs when you chose the order?
     —picked a deductive order for a reader who is opposed to your thesis?
     —picked an inductive order for all other readers?

SUMMARY

- There are compelling reasons to diagram your argument before you write a first draft
  —a diagram shows up flaws in the logic and structure of an argument
  —a diagram establishes the form of the argument
  —a diagram saves writing time by providing language for headings and text
- Each of the four diagram forms has special features
  —the organization tree shows relationships and flaws in logic. It is the natural development of the analysis tree and is easiest to use for descriptive reports.
  —the pyramid indicates the same relationships and flaws as the organization tree. It is the best way to picture the line of reasoning of a deductive argument.

—the linear outline is used traditionally and comes as second nature to some people, but it is less useful for checking logic than the tree or pyramid.

—the storyboard is especially useful for preparing an oral presentation and structuring sections of a long report, but it does not show the relationships in the full argument.

Case Study Exercise

Diagram the memo you have grouped and ordered for the **Complex** case or the **Budget** case. If you are accustomed to using a linear outline, try another form.

Further References

Kolb, Harold H. Jr. *A Writer's Guide: The Essential Points.* New York: Harcourt Brace Jovanovich, 1980.
Provides a simple illustration of the pyramid form as applied to paragraph structure. This book is the handiest short guide to writing (all forms) we have found.

Van Nostrand, A. D., et al. *Functional Writing.* Boston: Houghton Mifflin Co., 1977.
This book gives another version of the pyramid diagram.

6

BEGINNINGS AND ENDINGS: WHAT, WHY, AND HOW

The success or failure of your memo or report may very well depend on the first and last impressions the reader receives. This chapter will show you:

- How to write an introduction that will
  —get your reader interested
  —provide just enough information for an understanding of your argument
  —establish rapport with your reader
- How to close your argument and direct the reader to take action

Because they're so important, beginnings and endings warrant special care. It is not enough to charge ahead, making a bald statement of your recommendation or conclusion, piling up evidence, and then coming to an abrupt stop. One consultant we talked with insisted that he rewrites the first and last paragraph of each memo at least five times, even when he gets away with fewer drafts for the body. You can write more effective beginnings and endings the *first time* if you focus on the needs of the reader and follow the suggestions in this chapter.

Beginnings

Did you ever walk into a restaurant, look at the menu, and walk right out? Or, as we did once, taste the hors d'oeuvres and then ask for the bill? It is far easier for your reader to "walk out" on your memo than it is for you to walk out of the restaurant. The introduction's main function is to capture the reader's interest so he or she will keep on reading.

Attracting the Reader's Attention

To interest your readers, you must tell them what the memo or report is about, why it is important, and how you will develop your argument. The first point is obvious—a reader cannot become interested without knowing what the communication is about. Busy managers give their highest priority to material that directly relates to them, especially if it tells them how to do their jobs better or what action they must take. For this reason, the introduction should tell them, as early as possible, what's in it for them. Readers are also more likely to be interested if the introduction provides guidelines telling them how the report or memo will progress. If you do not give your readers a sense of direction, they will read aimlessly and retain little. Therefore, to interest the reader, an introduction must include:
- WHAT the report or memo is about
- WHY it is important to the reader
- HOW you will convey the message

Logically, you won't discuss the HOW until you've told the reader either what it's about or why it's important; you can deal with the WHAT and WHY in any order.

If you are asked to write a memo, it is reasonable to assume that the person making the request thinks the topic is important. In such cases, the introduction might be something simple like this:

> You asked me (WHY IMPORTANT) to analyze the techniques used at the Perkins plant (WHAT) to see if we could apply some of these methods to our operations. I have determined that we can adopt the following features: (HOW)

Pointing out initially that you are responding to a request from the reader should guarantee that you have his or her attention. The word *analyze* presents a clue that the subject of your investigation will follow, and it does: "techniques used at the Perkins plant." The clause, "we can adopt the following features," lets the reader know that a list will follow. Since this analysis is in response to a direct request, the body of the memo will also explain why you included each item on the list.

In most memos, and in any long report, a more explicit statement of the significance is necessary to entice the reader to continue. The following paragraph introduces a memo to the marketing director of a company:

> After five years of experience with Model K-22, we find that the machine has not reached the sales volume we anticipated. (WHAT) We believe this is detrimental to the total earnings picture of the firm. (WHY IMPORTANT) We have therefore reviewed the needs of corporations in all the markets in which the K-22 is sold to determine where we should put our marketing emphasis. (HOW)

This paragraph immediately indicates what the problem is (sales volume is below expectations), why it is a problem (it will affect earnings), and what the writer will consider in the remainder of the memorandum (how to market the product). The HOW portion suggests that a discussion of steps and the reasons for them will follow.

The following opening is from a magazine article directed to New England readers. The WHY would be different for another audience.

> Developers agree that the days of building Disney World style shopping centers are over. (WHAT) This is true not only because the costs of energy, construction, and land are soaring, but because of demo-

graphics. (HOW) New England, in particular, isn't growing fast enough to support any more megacenters. (WHY IMPORTANT)

Some people like to think of the introduction as a story that builds to a climax. Therefore, if you are writing a recommendation-first memo, you can often start with the WHY and lead into the WHAT. The HOW may be included where it seems most comfortable. In this kind of beginning, the closing sentence wows the reader with your recommendation, or punch line, which is the opening for the body of the communication:

> Earnings growth is threatened (WHY IMPORTANT) by the failure of Model K-22 to reach its sales potential. (WHAT) A study of the needs of the markets in which it is sold (HOW) indicates that our best opportunity is in the small-car field. We should concentrate our advertising efforts there.

You may feel that the best way to reach your reader is to give the punch line first:

> We should concentrate our efforts to sell Model K-22 in the small-car market. The failure of the model to meet its sales potential is threatening our earnings growth.

If you take this approach, however, you should make very certain that you have a friendly audience. If your readers vehemently disagree with your recommendation, and you give it away in the first sentence, they may not read the rest of your communication.

Look at the last report or memo you received. Is it clear from the introduction what the communication is about and why it is important to the reader? Are there guidelines for the reader that indicate how the argument will develop? When you write the introduction to your next report or memo, check to see that you have included all these elements.

Once you've attracted the reader's interest, your next task is to make sure the reader has enough information to understand the thrust of your argument but does not become mired in trivia.

Providing Just Enough Information

An introduction should include only those facts the primary reader and any important secondary readers need to understand the problem from your perspective. Anyone with young children knows that when the dinner table conversation is beyond their comprehension, most children will indicate their loss of interest by tuning out (or tossing the peas around). In the same way, a lecture on the geography of the Northeast will cause a child who asked, "When will we get to New York?" to gaze out the window and count beer cans by the side of the road. Successful communication can only occur when there is understanding. But using technical language with a generalist or explaining too much wastes time— yours and the reader's.

Although most of the examples in this chapter are very short, introductions to long reports may need to include historical or technical information if the reader is to understand the substance of the argument. Use your assessment of the background, knowledge, and preconceptions of the primary reader to determine the amount and technicality of the information you include.

Define your terms. Pay special attention to defining your terms, especially if the reader's responsibilities, experiences, educational background, or reading habits are significantly different from your own. Consider this opening paragraph of a consultant's report to clients:

> The recent accident at Three Mile Island has stimulated demands for severe cutbacks in the nation's nuclear power program. Costs should be an important element in determining whether such cutbacks are in the public interest. The EFG model provides a useful means of projecting costs given various restrictions on nuclear power development.

Acronyms and abbreviations are dangerous. Even if the primary reader can figure out what the EFG model is from the context, causing him or her to take time out to think about it will be an unnecessary distraction. If the reader doesn't know EFG from GNP, the point of the introduction will be lost. The full title of any bureau, board, commission, or similar organization should be spelled out the first time it is used (with the acronym or abbreviation following in parentheses) unless the audience for the report or memo could not possibly misunderstand:

> The Economic Forecast Group (EFG) model provides a useful means of projecting costs . . .

It is even possible that the reader is not familiar with the Three Mile Island incident or has forgotten it. If there's any doubt, build some words of explanation into the introduction:

> The recent accident at the Three Mile Island nuclear power plant, which might have produced extensive nuclear contamination, . . .

Such explanation is crucial if the report will sit in someone's file, to be referred to over a period of time.

All industries and professions have their own jargons. You can become so accustomed to hearing, speaking, and writing a particular jargon that you forget that others do not understand it. The writer of a report to the officers of a land trust fell into this trap when he wrote this sentence:

> Changing the residential zoning ordinances of the township to include a provision for average density cluster zoning seems possible from a legal point of view.

What is "average density cluster zoning"? Do all officers of the land trust understand this term? If there is any question that a reader will not fully understand a word or phrase, explain it.

The primary reader should know the meaning of every word in the introduction. If the audience is broad, assume that its members, while intelligent, lack technical knowledge of the subject. If secondary readers may not understand—and they are important—it is wise to define any questionable terms, either briefly in the text or, in a long report, in a footnote.

Explain the problem. Not only must every word be clearly defined, but the situation must be explained fully enough for the reader to comprehend the significance of the problem and the development of the analysis:

> With the competition for consumer deposits increasing as a result of the entry of thrifts into the third party payment side of the business, and with NOWs increasing the cost of maintaining such deposits, our efforts to retain and attract consumer deposits must be far more selective.

Let us assume that the reader knows that NOWs are Negotiable Orders of Withdrawal. How much does the writer need to say about thrifts? Should the writer have said, "savings banks and credit unions"? Is it necessary to make some comment about the way these institutions are encroaching upon the business of commercial banks? If the reader is the president of a commercial bank, the term *thrifts* should be enough to send shudders down his or her spine. If the audience is a group of the bank's loan officers, people who customarily spend their time disbursing funds to borrowers, and you want them to be concerned about attracting big depositors, you should give them some indication of the gravity of the situation:

> Since the entry of thrift institutions into the third party payment business, we have lost 10 percent of our deposits to such institutions. . . .

Indicate a shift in emphasis. Sometimes, when you've been asked to write, you find that your problem solving has led you to want to answer a question other than the one the reader asked. If that's the case, you should use your introduction to explain and justify your new approach. For example, the marketing director of a fast-food chain was asked by the president of the company to develop a marketing campaign for the southeastern part of the state modeled on a successful campaign the company had just completed in the western region. The marketing director was convinced that the real problem in the southeastern section was the public's reluctance to patronize stores in deteriorating neighborhoods. As a result, she wanted to change the question in the president's mind from "How can we best market the company in the southeast?" to the broader question, "What can we do about declining sales in the southeast?" Realizing that she couldn't ignore the original question or answer a new question without making the change in direction clear, the marketing director wrote this introduction:

> In reviewing the marketing strategy we recently used in the western region, I found that the campaign was most effective in areas where we have modern facilities and a middle-class population. In searching for similar communities in the southeast, I found only two. The vast majority of our stores there are in decaying neighborhoods. Store-by-store sales in the southeast show that we are doing well in the two towns where demographics match those in the west, but that sales are declining rapidly everywhere else.

The introduction deals with the president's original question but leads him to ask the question the marketing director wanted to answer, "What can we do about the declining sales?" In such cases it's important to prove in the body of the report that the shift in emphasis is justified.

State the criteria. If your report or memo is anything more than a description, the introduction is a good place to lay out the criteria for your decision or recommendation. In chapter 3 we presented the criteria for moving a small-parts plant to one of three locations: an adequate labor supply, location within twelve hours of the largest market, and low production costs. The introduction to a memo discussing those locations might begin like this:

> In view of our need to be within twelve hours of Tonnington, to limit production costs, and to have a supply of skilled labor . . .

The writer will further define the criteria when discussing alternatives in the body of the report. An "adequate" pool will be spelled out, and the costs at the three locations will be considered in terms of the other criteria. If this is a short memo, and the criteria are generally accepted by the reader, simply stating them should be sufficient. If it is a long report, no doubt the writer will want to expand on the criteria and justify the reasons for choosing them. The introduction should then include a section that develops the criteria and distinguishes limits of freedom from negotiable criteria.

> *Any report that does more than simply describe a situation or event must include a discussion of how well alternatives meet criteria. Are the criteria clearly stated in the introduction to the last nondescriptive report you wrote? Is it obvious which are limits of freedom? What about the last report or memo you received?*

Avoid "background." An effective introduction replaces the "background" section many writers feel obliged to include in their reports. Most traditional background sections are dull, and executives say they don't read them. We suspect that writers tend to fill these sections with tidbits of information for which they cannot find a logical home. Although many organizations consider these background sections sacred, we advise you not to include anything important in them if you have a choice in the matter. Your introduction is the place to tell the reader everything he or she needs to know to understand the argument.

The relatively long introduction below provides enough information to interest the principal reader, an investor who is not a stock-market specialist. Much of the information in the first paragraph might, in another memo, be put (and lost) in a section labeled "Background." Here the writer hammers home item after item about the unfavorable events that have caused investors to avoid stocks. By the end, the reader's attention should be nailed to the page in the hope that the writer will give some insight into ways to avoid personal financial disaster.

For much of this year, many investors have been building cash reserves with funds that might have been earmarked for stocks under more favorable circumstances, and they have done so for good reason. Inflation and interest rates have remained at extremely high levels; prices for gold and other precious metals have soared; the position of the United States dollar, although somewhat strengthened in relation to other leading currencies, remains tenuous at best; the energy situation, grimly reminiscent of the 1973–74 crisis, has worsened; and confidence in the administration's ability to deal effectively with the nation's problems has fallen to a new low. Moreover, with the growing consensus that a recession has begun, the major concern of investors—and market analysts—seems to have shifted to how lengthy and how deep the recession may be and how far corporate profits are likely to fall.

That concern, of course, is valid. Profits have always declined during recessions, and they can be expected to do so again. In fact, individual stocks have sold off sharply in recent trading sessions on news that earnings had failed to meet expectations. (WHY IMPORTANT)

At the same time, we believe that the recession has highly positive implications for the market. (WHAT) Historically, the market has seldom begun a sustained advance while interest rates were moving toward a peak, and interest rates have dropped only when economic activity has weakened significantly. (HOW) In our judgment, the recession moves us one step closer to the time when equities should again provide returns that are greater than those available on alternative investments. (WHAT restated)

The skeptical reader of this introduction may well question the writer's conclusion that stocks will soon be a better investment than the other alternatives, and the body of the text should therefore include support for this argument. If you can safely assume the reader will agree with the conclusion at once, or if you have been asked *how* to do something, use the introduction to provide the minimum information about What, Why, and How, and include in the body of the text only the steps you expect to take. Such action-oriented reports are very effective.

Review for too little or too much. Because introductions are so important, always review yours to be certain they contain neither too little nor too much. For example, this beginning is clearly inadequate, as well as dull:

> The purpose of this memo is to consider sales goals and projections for the department and for individual salesmen.

The reader, unless psychic, has no idea why reading this report is important. Something like this would be more useful:

> As part of the long range planning process, we have used the corporation's economic forecasts to develop departmental and individual sales goals. We have compared these with our most recent sales projections and found that the goals are unrealistic.

On the other hand, this introduction (part of which was cited earlier) has both too much and too little:

> Changing the residential zoning ordinances of the township to include a provision for average density cluster zoning seems possible from a legal point of view. The case law suggests that cluster zoning is a valid exercise of the police power under the state enabling legislation. It has been instituted in three townships, A, B, and C, and there have been no challenges. Although I do not believe cluster zoning is the panacea, from a planning point of view, that it was held to be ten years ago, it appears to be an appropriate tool to preserve open space and control the density of the population both from your point of view and from the town's.

As we said before, "average density cluster zoning" provides too little information and should be defined. On the other hand, the fact that there are three towns in which no legal challenge has taken place is supporting evidence for the assertion that this form of zoning is legal. As such, it does not belong in the introduction. If the purpose of the memo is to support the argument that cluster zoning is legal, a discussion of the towns in which it has not been challenged belongs in the body of the report. This introduction fails to tell the reader the purpose, or the WHAT, of the report. The writer also does not make clear whether he intends to provide guidelines for developing acceptable and useful ordinances. Here is one possible way of rewriting the introduction to answer these objections:

> Average density cluster zoning, which would concentrate residential structures in small portions of a subdivision, would both preserve open spaces and control the town's population density. Changing the town ordinances to include a provision for such zoning can be done within the law if we conform to the requirements set forth in the cases reviewed below, and if we consider carefully those issues not yet tested in the courts.

Establishing Rapport With the Reader

The tone you adopt in the introduction depends on your working and personal relationship with the reader. If you asked a co-worker who is also a friend to read and evaluate one of your reports, you would probably feel offended if it came back with a note beginning, "Your report is returned herewith." Wouldn't you rather receive a note that begins, "I found your report most interesting"? Yet normally friendly people often freeze into formality when writing. On the other hand, if a communication is directed to superiors, informality is inappropriate. You would not begin a memo to your boss with "Joe, when I saw you at the bar last night I remembered . . ." You can avoid errors in tone by keeping your relationship with the reader in mind as you write.

Since the introduction should establish a common ground and prepare your reader to accept your argument, it should contain only information with which the reader is likely to agree. If you have bad news, save it for the body of the report, where you may choose to state it before or after the positive information. To get something out in the open quickly may be emotionally satisfying, but you risk losing your audience altogether. Remember, the purpose of the introduction is to keep the reader with you.

> *Did the introduction to the last memo you wrote "sound" as if you were talking to the reader? Did it indicate the relationship you wanted to establish? Did the introduction prepare the reader to accept what followed? Did it encourage the reader to move along with you as an attentive listener rather than as an antagonist?*

We have said a great deal about writing good introductions because they are both extremely important and difficult to write. The writer of an introduction makes a contract with the reader: "I will now tell you, as pleasantly as possible, exactly what, why, and how." The success or failure of the report or memo largely depends on whether the writer keeps the contract.

Endings

In *Alice's Adventures in Wonderland*, the King tells the White Rabbit, ". . . go on till you come to the end; then stop." To apply this advice to reports or memos, simply avoid belaboring the point once you have completed the argument. Except for very short memos, however, the ending has a definite purpose. To be effective, it should:
- Provide a sense of closure
- Summarize the important points
- Set out the next step

In addition, endings must never include new information about the problem you have discussed. If the assertion is important, it belongs in the body of the text. If it is not important, forget it.

Providing a Sense of Closure

A cliff-hanger makes readers uncomfortable and frustrated. Suppose you came to the end of a memo about an advertising premium campaign and read this:

> We estimate that the proposed campaign will be less than 30 percent effective. This estimation may be high when we consider that we are entering the low-consumption winter season.

So what if the estimate is high? What is the significance of a 30 percent effectiveness rate? How about:

> We estimate that, in spite of its low dollar outlay, the proposed premium campaign will be less than 30 percent effective and does not compare, in terms of payback, with the free-sample campaign recommended last week.

The second example indicates the significance of the 30 percent effectiveness rate and suggests something that might take the place of the premium promotion. It gives a sense of finality to discussion of the promotion.

Summarizing

In a memo of two pages or less, a summary ending should not be necessary, especially if the recommendation or conclusion is visually highlighted by bullets or underlining at the beginning of the memo. (See chapter 8 for more on graphic design.) In fact, in a very short report, you insult a reader's intelligence by summarizing. In a long report, however, the ending should summarize your thinking on the subject—it should reinforce the major points you want the reader to remember. This is your last chance to get your message across:

> The strategy we have outlined here may be divided into three parts: we have established plans to provide for our space needs during the next three months while construction is underway; we have detailed plans to meet our needs for the next five years; and we have developed long-range projections based on our anticipated growth. We will therefore be able to review our needs at each stage.

This ending summarizes the material that preceded and indicates how it can be used.

Setting Out the Next Step

Since most management reports and memos are written to initiate some action, the most effective ending tells the reader exactly what to do next to put the recommendation into motion. After reading the following paragraph, the company's president knew exactly what to do to implement the consultant's recommendations:

> The keys to the future success of our organization will be to institute the action plans set out above and to modify these plans as the environment changes. This proposal presents a major challenge but one that can be met if the board appoints a committee composed of several members of the senior management staff to oversee the program, review the timetable, and consider necessary changes on a regular basis.

The best-conducted ending also creates an opportunity for

direct communication between writer and reader and establishes
a time for action:

> John and I will be guiding you through this installation. Nevertheless,
> it is important that you establish a good accounting system before we
> begin. We will be glad to meet with you Friday to begin planning for
> such a system.

The time you take to write a good ending is always well spent,
for a good ending will leave the reader believing you are compe-
tent and your argument is valid.

*Look at the endings of some memos and reports you wrote recently.
Do they come to a close or do they leave the reader with an
incomplete thought? Does the reader know what to do next? Have
you really hit the jackpot and set some time at which something
will happen?*

SUMMARY

- An introduction should
  —interest the reader
  —provide enough information for the reader to understand the
    logic of the argument
  —establish rapport
- To interest the reader, every introduction should include
  —WHAT the report or memo is about
  —WHY it is important to the reader
  —HOW you will convey the message
- To provide just enough information, the introduction should
  —explain the problem
  —indicate any shift in emphasis
  —establish the criteria
- The writer establishes rapport with the reader in the introduction through
  —an appropriate tone
  —acceptable content
- Endings should provide a sense of completion and leave the
  reader with something to do
- The ending of a long report or memo should summarize the
  argument

Case Study Exercises ───────────────────

Usually you write your entire first draft all at once. Because opening statements are so important, however, you should do the following exercises for additional practice:

1. **Complex.** Write the introduction of the memo you would write if you were Russo writing to top management. Indicate the WHAT, WHY IMPORTANT, and HOW.

2. **Budget.** Write the introduction to the memo you would write if you were Lerue writing to the investment committee. Indicate WHAT, WHY IMPORTANT, and HOW.

Further References ───────────────────

Shurter, Robert L., Williamson, J. Peter, and Broehl, Wayne G., Jr. *Business Research and Report Writing*. New York: McGraw-Hill, 1965.
Chapter 9 gives several good examples of both opening statements and conclusions, as well as a general discussion of principles.

7

WRITING THE FIRST DRAFT

All your hard work on organization will now pay off in writing the first draft. This chapter will show you:
- How to pick the best writing format
- How to present a long report
- How to get started and keep writing
- How to check your first draft to be sure it meets the reader's needs

When asked how the book on his days as a power-broker was coming, Henry Kissinger commented: "Writing is hell. And it's a lonely enterprise." Kissinger had three researchers and four secretaries to help relieve his loneliness. Although you don't have a staff to help you write, the logical argument you developed in the first part of the book should make you feel less alone. Effective writing depends on high-quality content and imaginative packaging. Organizing has helped you gain control of your content. This chapter will suggest ways to present the argument attractively and persuasively.

Presentation, or packaging, includes the format, the words you use, stylistic devices, and any visuals you design to illustrate your main points. Properly used, these elements indicate your self-confidence, intelligence, and understanding of the reader's position. The place to begin is with the first draft.

Choosing a Format

Many large organizations have standard formats. Some stipulate the order in which sections appear. Some (not enough) give guidelines about length. Some even provide fat style manuals giving very detailed rules. The U.S. Army, for instance, gives a rule for handling paragraphs that cannot be concluded on the bottom of a page—"Do not divide a paragraph of three lines or less."

Standard formats often make things easier for the reader. People accustomed to reading reports that follow a standard format save time because they know where to look for specific kinds of information. Using a standard format saves the writer's time because relying on a familiar formula requires fewer decisions than devising an original design.

But, using a standard format is more like painting by numbers than it is like painting the ceiling of the Sistine Chapel—creativity is sacrificed to ease. It's all too simple to fall back on statements like "We're supposed to do it this way" when, in fact, "this way" is nothing more than poor style reinforced by habit. If your organization has a standard format, don't stray from it unless you have a good reason. If no guidelines exist, however, you may be in a better position to tailor your memo or report to the needs of the reader and the content of the document.

If you are writing for a one-page-only reader, you will want to get all the important information on that page by using a modified outline form, an executive summary, or both. If you are writing for someone who wants to read the concepts and let his or her staff review the data, you will probably write a brief report and collect all the supporting evidence in a separate section. If you are seeking to draw attention to a problem, you may want to depart from your usual format to emphasize the originality of your argument. Managers who receive stacks of memos every week may overlook important information if it looks just like all the unimportant information that arrives daily.

Given the leeway to choose your own format, then, you will select the one that best conveys the information in a way that is most useful and pleasing to the reader. If you are writing a memo, you may choose a modified outline or prose format. If you are writing a long report, you will need to decide on the placement and length of certain information and sections.

Modified Outline versus Prose Format

The modified outline format is becoming increasingly popular in business and government. It makes heavy use of bullets and dashes to indicate major points. Frequently, major points are written as full sentences, but transitions are kept to a minimum. A memo in this form is concise and requires less time to write than one in paragraph form. Consider the following example (which would be only one segment of an actual memo), and mentally compare it with the paragraph we might have written instead:

A memo in modified outline form
- Permits the reader to
  —quickly identify important points
  —see the relationship between points
- Requires the writer to
  —eliminate nonessential information
  —order the information logically
  —leave out such stylistic niceties as similes and metaphors
  —leave out transitions

As you can see, the modified outline form provides a strong visual statement of your argument. For this reason, it is effective for writing reports and memos that emphasize a few important points or for organizing a long report in conjunction with an oral presentation. In the latter case, the outline form reinforces the major points the author wants remembered; complex material can be talked through; and the written document serves as a useful reference. Although the example given here is not written in full sentences, important or major points should often be in full-sentence form to avoid confusing a reader or permitting a speaker to lose track of the arguments for an oral presentation.

Several considerations may work against using the modified outline. First, its abbreviated language is far from elegant. Stripping the memo of all examples, analogies, and detail may destroy a reader's incentive to keep going. Second, because the form does not allow amplification, the reader may fail to grasp some of the more subtle points. For this reason, the modified outline form should be used only when extended support for the argument is not necessary or may be put in an appendix. Third, using the modified outline form for an entire memo lessens the impact of the bullets. Reading such a memo is just as dull as wading through page after page of unbroken print. Fourth, some readers perceive the writer of a modified outline memo as "coming on strong" and may ignore the content because they're offended by the form. You'll want to weigh the advantages and disadvantages before choosing the modified outline.

Can you use the modified outline format in a memo or report you are writing now? Try it and see what you think.

How to Present a Long Report

Reports are more formal documents than memos and usually follow a fairly conventional scheme. They are generally accompanied by a letter of transmittal (or memorandum, if the report is not for public use), which tells the recipient why the report is significant. A long report includes the following:

Report Format

Title page
Gives name of organization, title of report, date, and name of writer or writers.

Executive summary
Provides an overview of the contents of the report. This

should include a statement of the problem, the major criteria, the recommendation, and some supporting evidence.

Table of Contents (or **Contents**)
Gives the main divisions of the report and page numbers.

Body
Includes an introduction, the findings or results of the research, and the conclusions. The introduction, in this case, will be longer than for a short memo. It will probably include some historical material, since the readership of a long report is generally larger than that of a memo or short report, and because a long report frequently serves as a reference over a period of time. The introduction will often include a section on criteria, and may include a list of assumptions on which critical findings were based.

The findings may appear in abbreviated form, with the bulk of the results in the appendixes, or they may be expanded upon in detail in the text. Again, this depends on whether the material demands extensive explanation and what approach the primary reader prefers. Sometimes conclusions are put in the recommendation section, but most often they are in the body of the document as the natural development of the findings.

Recommendations
May precede or follow the body of the report.

Glossary
Provides definitions of terms (primarily for technical reports).

Appendixes and Exhibits
Provide the detailed data that support the findings.

Reports differ, of course, depending on their purpose and the position of the writer vis-a-vis the reader. If you are attempting to create a format from scratch, looking at the reports and style manuals of organizations similar to yours will help.

For your own sake, you should decide on a format before you begin to write. Changing your mind part way through the first draft is a waste of time.

Beginning to Write

We have all heard of novelists who write and rewrite an opening sentence, never getting it quite perfect and never writing anything more. The hardest part of writing is getting something, anything, on paper. Unlike the novelist, you have a good deal of the final document *already written.* Now, all the work you have done getting ready to write will pay off. The conclusion, recommendation, or thesis statement, already in sentence form and ready to use, is on the left branch of your organization tree or the top box of the pyramid. Each of the section headings is written at the next level of whatever diagram you have used. You have stated the criteria accurately and have written down the reasons for each. Your supporting data are entered on note cards and the cards are grouped and ordered, waiting only for you to flip through them, picking up what you need as you write. For you, writing the first draft is nothing more than stringing together the parts you have already prepared. If you had writing anxiety before, you should not have it now. Managers who follow this method agree that writing, at this stage, is simple. Your job now is to get started—and keep yourself going.

How to Keep Going

How you get going and keep going depends on who you are. But whoever you are, writing takes concentration, and it pays to establish an environment that will discourage distractions. Time and efficiency managers insist on the importance of setting aside a block of time in which to write. They maintain that trying to write during the small stretches of time you find between phone calls and walk-in conversations is wasteful; it takes too long to go back and reorganize your thoughts after each interruption.

A scientist-writer we know claims he does his best work while traveling. He tells a story about sitting for two hours on a plane parked at the end of a runway: "I got more writing done in those two hours than in a week in the office. No one bothered me." One executive vice-president gets his best writing done in his office from seven to nine in the morning when no one else is around. Even after the rest of the staff arrives, the momentum he has built up carries him through their interruptions. Many professional writers work all night, and so do some executives. Then there are those of us who work best when the office quiets down after five, and we can postpone going home to make dinner.

Creating a conducive mind-set is part of establishing the right environment. Some people write best after warming up. Zealous joggers don't just open the front door and start running. They get themselves ready with ten or fifteen minutes of stretching exercises and sit-ups and then walk for a quarter mile or so before they step up the pace. If you aren't fighting an impossible deadline, you may find that gradualism will help you relax and write with more energy. Try reading a short magazine article on an unrelated topic that interests you. Savor the way the author gets his or her points across in print. Surprisingly, this will often give you a creative approach to a thorny writing problem. Then write something short and satisfying—a letter congratulating a friend on a promotion, for example. This step is particularly important when you're writing a long report and won't get any rewards until the tedious job is over. The whole warming-up process should not take more than ten or fifteen minutes.

Whatever you do to get started, you will want to provide a mental sanctuary from intrusions. Think for a few minutes about where, when, and how you do your most productive work. If you can discover what kind of environment motivates you to start writing and keep going, you can strive to create a situation as close to it as possible.

Setting Manageable Goals

Once you've established a motivating environment, you need to set reasonable goals for yourself. These goals should be attainable but remote enough that you will not be able to put off working toward them. One report writer we know will not leave the office until he has completed the five pages of typescript he expects to write each day. If he is inspired to write more than five pages on one day, he still writes at least five pages the next. In this way he is able to finish a fifty-page report in two working weeks. We suggest that, whenever possible, you use the following process to set goals before you begin.

Guidelines for Setting a Writing Schedule

1. Establish the final deadline for the report.

2. Set your personal deadline two days earlier (nothing goes as quickly as you think it will).

3. Allow time to have the report typed. Add a day for proof-reading and corrections.

4. Set aside time for revising.

5. Divide the remaining time among problem solving, fact finding, organizing, and writing the first draft.

6. Set a timetable and stick to it.

Picking the Right Method

Whether you dictate the report, write it out in longhand, or type it is a matter of personal preference and the availability of equipment. Writing longhand is a slow process. Most people who use this method do so because it is easy to go back and make changes. Some executives tell us that writing in longhand helps them think and keeps them closer to the project. We suspect that a preference for this method is primarily a matter of habit.

Composing at the typewriter is an acquired skill, but there are reasons for learning to do it. If your handwriting is less than terrific, life will be much easier for your secretary when drafts are readable. Words and sentences look different in print; errors and lapses are easier to see. And once you get used to it, writing on the typewriter is much faster than writing longhand.

Any manager should also to learn to dictate efficiently. The immense savings in time makes it worthwhile. Most people write about ten words per minute; the usual dictation speed is sixty words per minute. In addition, the ability to dictate succinct messages will be more and more in demand as portable dictating machines become more sophisticated, stenographers become rarer, and computerized typing of spoken messages becomes more feasible.

Dictated copy has the potential advantage of sounding more natural than written copy because talking is more natural than writing. Of course, "talking it" may also result in irritating repetition of phrases like "you know" or "of course" and the use of slang. It's easy enough to eliminate these problems during revision, however. Remember that no one gets it right the first time.

Many managers don't dictate because they're embarrassed or uncomfortable about the process. Dictating effectively is a skill that can only be acquired through practice. If you're a novice at dictating, think small in the beginning. Start with a short letter on a familiar subject, move to memos, and ultimately graduate to sections of long reports. The following suggestions will help you dictate more efficiently:

Guidelines for Dictating

1. Use outlines to guide you.

2. Before you start the first paragraph, indicate what kind of communication it is—a memo, a letter, a long report? A draft or final copy? About how long? What kind of paper?

3. Dictate capitalization, punctuation, paragraphing. Spell out names, words that sound like other words, and words that have more than one spelling.

4. When you are making comments to the typist (corrections or instructions), be certain they are not confused with your text. We have all seen embarrassing asides that appeared in the final copy.

5. If you dictate afterthoughts at the end of a tape, leave written instructions about their insertion in the text.

6. Read and correct everything you dictate. Remember, the author, not the secretary, is responsible for the final copy.

7. Don't be afraid to dictate draft copy for later revision. Most secretaries would rather type from a tape than decipher an illegibly written draft.

Where to Begin

Some writing consultants argue that one should begin by writing the conclusions. Some insist that the findings should be written first. A writer we know always constructs her exhibits first (following her working outline); one consulting firm's handbook flatly states that making the exhibits first is the sign of an amateur. Writing the findings or making the charts and tables first helps you pull the data together and exposes any yawning chasms in the supporting evidence. But some writers need to know what they said in the beginning in order to go on. If you are a first-things-first writer, you should follow your inclinations. The more natural you feel about writing, the easier it will be for you—and the better the final result. Good arguments, however, can be made for beginning with either the body or the conclusion.

If the report or memo is short or informal, you may plunge right in, writing the body of the text or the support for your argument first. Since you have most of this on paper already, it is probably the easiest place to begin. Once something is on paper, the rest tends to come more readily. Writing the summary of a long report first has several advantages. A good summary states the problem, the conclusion, and the major premises that support the conclusion. If you can look at your summary and say, "That is a good, logical argument," you are well on the way to writing a good, full report. Writing the summary first forces you to eliminate extraneous ideas and gives you excellent practice in writing concise prose. In addition, you can refer to your summary as you review the full report to be sure you did not go off on a tangent as you wrote. If you are unwilling to write the summary first, check your motive—you may be unsure of the conclusion. When you write the summary last, it is very tempting merely to provide a digest of what you have already put on paper, rather than to summarize your thinking about the subject.

What you write first is your choice—pick the part that is most comfortable for you.

Guidelines for First Drafts

Although you should not feel constrained by rules when you are writing a first draft (the point is to get something on paper), it's obvious that a good first draft minimizes the need for revision. Following a few pointers developed with the reader in mind can help you write an effective first draft. Once again, picture your reader as an intelligent person who nevertheless needs guidance in following your argument.

First Draft Guidelines

1. Be natural.

2. Set up the reader's expectations.

3. Review and preview regularly.

4. Construct your paragraphs intelligently.

5. Don't make assertions unless you draw inferences from them.

6. Don't skip steps.

7. Elaborate on the unusual.

8. Use examples and be specific.

9. Stay with the diagram.

10. Keep writing.

---

1. Be natural. Trying to write as if you were someone else (presumably someone more important, more educated, or more sophisticated) will lead to stilted sentences and a stiff, leaden tone. Your major decision is whether to use the first person singular, *I*, and the second person singular, *you*. We recommend that you use both whenever appropriate.

It is obviously appropriate to use the first and second person singular when you are writing to someone you know, as you usually are in a short memo. Going into convolutions (passive voice, use of impersonal *one*) to avoid it is not only silly, but is also a barrier to clarity. For example, if you are dealing with quantities of data, some of which have already been partially digested by other groups (outside consultants, for instance), there are vast differences in meaning among:

> My analysis of the data shows . . .
> The consultants' analysis of the data shows . . . *and*
> Analysis of the data shows . . . *(Whose analysis are you talking about?)*

When you are writing a formal report, you will usually use the third person or, unfortunately, the passive voice; unless you are a senior executive, you are most often writing for someone else's signature. However, if you have the opportunity, write in the first person. The passive is dull and the third person, unless you are adept, sounds foolish:

> The author's *(referring to yourself)* analysis shows . . .

In some cases you may be able to use the first person plural, *we,* if the report will be signed by several individuals or an organizational group.

2. Set up the reader's expectations. Readers find what they expect to find. Therefore, as in your introduction, sections and subsections should always indicate what you want the reader to look for. If you clearly are going to discuss personnel problems, the reader will not look for production issues. A reader who knows you are going to explain several problems will look for more than one and will make a mental note at each major point—an aid to remembering the argument. Moreover, the reader will find it gratifying to successfully collect all the points you promise. You say, "You can improve your sales in four ways." As you cite the fourth method, the reader thinks, "Ah, now I have all four." We have used numbers here; two of this, three of that. But an unending line of "first," "second," and so forth can be numbing. Don't use the device wantonly.

3. Review and preview. You should remind the reader of the direction of the argument. Not, however, by talking about topics— "This section contains a discussion of the problem and recommendations for immediate change"—but by indicating the substance of the discussion:

> Achieving Atlantic's major goals of increasing sales and cutting costs
> will require significant effort. The programs described in this section

are designed to build on current strengths, focus on areas of potential improvement, and provide a system of periodic review.

Reminded that increasing sales and cutting costs are goals, the reader will now look for programs to accomplish those goals.

4. Construct your paragraphs intelligently. A paragraph without structure is as meaningless to a reader as a document that has no organization. A paragraph should be a unit of thought. Readers expect all the thoughts in a paragraph to relate to one central issue or idea and their minds tend to idle or race furiously when they have to work to figure out what the main idea is. Can you follow the logic of this argument?

> Our competition, the original equipment manufacturers (OEMs), not only have the necessary resources to formulate entire service packages, they could adapt our machines to their systems. These large OEMs dominate the market. They set the pace. They will not buy our machine unless there is a strong demand from end users. The end users will not buy the machine from us because they believe it is not yet functional.

What is the central idea of this paragraph? Is the writer trying to support the assertion that our competition can adapt our machine to their system? Is he or she trying to prove that the OEMs dominate the market? That neither they nor the end users will buy our product? What is the relationship among the ideas? It is impossible to revise this paragraph without knowing the answers to these questions.

We recommend that you construct your paragraphs from the "top down," as you have done for the total memo or report. Managers skim. Additionally, a number of speed-reading courses teach students to read only first and last sentences of paragraphs. If you want to be certain you are understood, it is best to begin with the sentence that tells the reader what the rest of the paragraph is about. You should be able to take your topic sentences directly from your diagram and fill in the rest of the paragraph with the data or evidence you have to support that statement.

You may wish, occasionally, to use a deductive order and put the topic sentence last, when it is necessary to follow the steps in order to understand the point. In such cases, the first sentence of the paragraph must still be an attention-getter in order to keep the reader with you:

> The American public now spends 10 percent of the GNP on medical care. Of that 10 percent, the greatest proportion goes toward maintaining patients with catastrophic illnesses (those that cost an individual over $5,000 in any given year). Catastrophic illnesses can only be paid for through major medical insurance. Therefore, this insurance is important for every member of our staff.

In a report on the insurance needs of employees, this first sentence will focus the reader's attention on the need for medical insurance, although the last sentence is the topic sentence.

We have no particular aversion to one-sentence paragraphs. Remember, however, that a one-sentence paragraph will emphasize the thought it expresses and thereby de-emphasize everything else on the page; make sure that the quality or importance of the thought warrants that treatment. Overusing one-sentence paragraphs, like overusing any other technique that emphasizes, will defeat your purpose.

5. Don't make assertions unless you draw inferences from them. The reader should not have to guess at your meaning; you should make the meaning and the significance clear. If there is any question that the reader might say, "so what?" or "why?" you should indicate the inference you expect him or her to draw:

> Both our sailcloth suppliers have closed down for two weeks this August. As a result, we are falling behind in deliveries *(why is this important?)* and will not be able to meet our commitments for the Marblehead to Halifax race.

It is now clear to the reader, who is waiting for a sail, that he will be out of luck. It would have been even clearer had the writer said, "Therefore, we may not be able to make your new mainsail."

6. Don't skip steps. If you have ever put together a child's toy on Christmas Eve, you know what we mean. The writer of the instructions understood that in order to put part A together with part B it is necessary to bend the end of part A thirty degrees. But you, the reader, do not know this unless you are told. If your document requires that you explain steps, or if the logic of your argument is dependent upon a series of events or thoughts, don't leave any out.

7. Elaborate on the unusual. The compare/contrast technique helps keep the reader's interest. Why is your proposal different from so many others that come across the executive's desk? What is it about the solution that is especially applicable to this problem?

8. Use examples and be specific. You can save paragraphs of vague description with one pointed example. If you've been asked to assess the quality of a new management-by-objectives program, for instance, one example showing that a particular manager's goals are unfocused and unmeasurable will do more to convince the CEO that there is a need for additional training than five pages of generalizations.

Although general statements are important (no one, remember, can tolerate a blow-by-blow description of every detail of a problem), specifics make them meaningful. In a monthly report that says, "The sales force had a productive month," adding, "In March, our sixteen travellers made a total of 400 calls, resulting in 210 orders" makes the claim much more convincing.

9. Stay with the diagram. This does not mean you have to resist the urge to add an idea that occurs to you as you are writing. As we all know, writing is not a linear process. You must, however, first plug any new thought into your diagram to make certain it fits. You have worked hard constructing a tight, logical argument. It would be foolish to lose your reader through the introduction of extraneous thoughts. If you find you don't like the diagram, by all means change it. But don't put it in the desk and forget it.

10. Keep writing. This is most important. If you can't think of just the right word, put down another one and keep going. Or leave a blank to fill in later. If you have an idea to add to a section a few pages back, make a note in the margin and keep writing. If you stop to go back to rewrite in the first draft, you may lose your train of thought. Always keep writing until you've met your quota of pages for the day.

> *How many of the suggestions in the First Draft guidelines do you naturally follow? Check yourself on the next report you write. Look especially for thesis sentences, and previewing and reviewing.*
> *List the guidelines you failed to follow, and read the list before you start to write next time.*

SUMMARY

- Before you start to write you must decide
  —whether to use a modified outline or paragraph format
  —what sections to include in a long report and their order
- Writing an effective first draft requires that you
  —choose an environment that encourages you to write

—set goals based on the available time and stick to them
- Which section you write first is less important than getting something on paper
- Keeping the needs of the reader in mind as you write will minimize your need to rewrite
  —whenever possible, use the first person singular
  —set up and meet expectations
  —tell the reader what you have just said and what you will say next
  —be sure paragraphs are well constructed around one main idea, which is the first or the last sentence
  —indicate the inference you expect the reader to draw from each assertion
  —don't skip steps
  —elaborate on the unusual
  —use examples and be specific
  —write from your diagram
  —keep writing

Case Study Exercises

1. **Complex.** Write the first draft of the memo you would write if you were Russo (a) writing to top management or (b) to Pilawski.

2. **Budget.** Write the first draft of the memo you would write if you were Lerue preparing to go to the investment committee. This draft should be in modified outline form.

Further References

Olson, Gene. *Sweet Agony: A Writing Manual of Sorts.* Grants Pass, OR: Windyridge Press, 1972.
The first three chapters give useful advice on overcoming writing anxiety and getting started.

Trimble, John R. *Writing with Style.* Englewood Cliffs, NJ: Prentice-Hall, 1975.
Although aimed primarily at college students, Trimble's advice on overcoming anxiety and writing first drafts is valuable for anyone who writes.

Zinsser, William. *On Writing Well.* New York: Harper and Row, 1979.
One of the best-loved books on writing. Easy and fun to read.

8
DESIGN FOR EMPHASIS

Designing your memo or report to emphasize your points and constructing visuals that support your arguments are important packaging techniques. This chapter will help you:

- Find the right graphic design for your memo or report through sensible use of
  —bulleting
  —underlining
  —capitalizing
  —headlining
- Construct effective visuals that
  —emphasize conclusions you draw from your facts
  —organize and efficiently present complex data

According to one management consultant, "The span of attention of the average $200,000-a-year executive is half a page." Getting a busy executive to concentrate on a report or memo is a challenge to any writer.

Designing the Report or Memo

Stylistic devices such as bullets, underlining, capitals, and headings can help focus the reader's attention because they:
- Reinforce the main points
- Emphasize the logical development of the argument
- Break up long sections of type and improve the appearance of a page

Reinforcing the Main Points

In any short memo and in any section of a long report, most of the text is supporting evidence, and there are only one or two main points that the writer wants the reader to remember. These are the points that set the structure for the material that follows, show the development of the argument, or summarize the preceding text. Setting these points off from the body of the text underscores their importance.

Compare the following conclusions:

To achieve this goal we recommend that you allocate $100,000 to permit rapid identification of alternatives to coffee and quicker development of selected products.

To achieve this goal we recommend that you allocate $100,000 to:
- Allow more rapid identification of alternatives to coffee
- Permit quicker development of selected products

Bullets, underlining, and capitals pull the reader to your major points. The device you choose depends on the nature of the point you want to make.

Bullets are most effective when you want to emphasize more than one assertion and when the statements are one line or less. They may be used with longer statements in a modified outline memo. Bullets are very effective when used in an opening statement to indicate the topics to be discussed in a report or memo. Examine the following introduction:

Although we have made great strides in the last five years by capitalizing on the use of new technology and improving efficiency, to produce significant savings we must still:
- Computerize the input, storage, and output of data
- Restructure our operations along functional lines

This opening statement clearly tells the reader what the two
most important areas for savings are and how the report will be
ordered—the discussion of computerization will precede the discussion of restructuring. Try this technique the next time you write
a short memo. It will improve both the clarity and punch of your
first paragraph.

Underlining is another way of attracting the reader's attention. It
is especially appropriate when the statement is long and when you
believe that the reader may miss the salient point if it is submerged
in a paragraph of complex or technical supporting evidence. When
you are underlining a series of ideas in one section, <u>all ideas that
are underlined must be equally important and at the same level of
abstraction.</u> To underline a major point and then to underline
supporting points as well would confuse the reader and distract
from, rather than emphasize, the primary argument. In a short
memo, underlined sentences can replace section headings when
the main argument cannot be reduced to a short caption.

Capitalization, as a stylistic device, can be effectively used to des-
ignate items in a series. In this excerpt from an advertising department memo, ignore the fact that the jargon-filled prose is only
understandable to a sailing fanatic:

Over the past five years technological advances have enabled us to
produce three variations on the highly successful Cassona 40.

The MARK II is a high-aspect ratio boat that goes well to weather
and has a proven racing record.

The MARK III was designed for the cruising sailor who is more
interested in ease of handling and likes a split rig.

The MARK IV is our latest development and has been designed
largely for use in the Transpac race, in which downwind work is most
important.

The use of capitals in this example is attractive and appropriate.
It indicates that all the items are a variation on one theme. Full
sentences or long phrases of text in capital letters, however, sug-

gest a strident writer. Of course, using capitalization for emphasis is pointless in documents containing acronyms for government agencies or corporations.

Helping the Reader Follow the Argument

Headings, like bullets, underlining, and capitals, attract the reader's attention and break up the text. In addition, they serve as guideposts, alerting readers that a new subject is beginning and telling them how that subject relates to other parts of the memo or report. Intelligently written headings also show the reader the framework of the argument. Since many managers read only headings, a wise writer uses them to make major points. Usually, you can borrow the headings from your diagram or outline of the argument. Try to keep headings short.

If your organization does not specify heading styles, you can develop your own style by following these rules:

- Each heading and subheading should meaningfully describe the material that follows
- Each heading should be understandable by itself
- Within each section, headings on the same level of generalization should be parallel in structure
- Headings should follow a consistent format

Headings Create Expectations. Headings create expectations by indicating the ideas that follow. Labels like "Background," "Summary," and "Considerations," although they break up the text, do not tell the reader anything about the argument. In a report dealing with the use of toxic substances in fertilizers, for example, "Short-range considerations" and "Long-range considerations" are less valuable headings than "Interim steps can reduce toxicity" and "Long-range plans will eliminate toxicity."

Headings Must Stand Alone. Each heading should be understandable without reference to the text, so that a reader skimming the memo or report can be carried along by the headings. Every heading should therefore contain a verb from which the direction of the discussion can be deduced. (Active verbs provide better signals than passive verbs or forms of the verb *to be*.) Furthermore, headings should not contain terms that are defined in the text that follows. For the report comparing the three locations to which the company might move its small-parts assembly (the argument is shown as an organization tree in chapter 5), you might use the following section headings:

     Location C is closest to our primary market
     Location C has the least costly labor supply
     Location C minimizes our capital expenditures

Subheadings under "Location C minimizes our capital expenditures" might be:

     Municipality will issue industrial development bonds
     Municipality will develop power project

If, in the same example, you are discussing alternatives and are not making a direct recommendation, you could base the headings on criteria:

     Proximity to the market is crucial
     Labor costs should be minimized
     Capital expenditures should be limited

Headings Should Be Parallel. Headings and subheadings *beneath any one heading* should be parallel in form. This simply means that the headings for closely related sections should be similar in structure to show that they are related. Headings for a discussion of steps in a process might look like this:

     Evaluate forging plant operations
     Review assembly line procedures
     Reassess advertising campaign

All these headings contain active verbs. The following group of headings is awkward:

     Evaluate forging plant operations
     Review assembly line procedures
     Reassessment of advertising campaign

Furthermore, use of a noun in the last head suggests that the third section does not relate to the first two. Readers often look for parallel structure as one of the clues to relationships.

Headings Should Follow a Consistent Format. The location on a page and the type size of headings indicate the importance of the subject to the reader. A misplaced heading sends the reader an incorrect message. Inconsistencies indicate that the writer does not pay sufficient attention to detail. To avoid any confusion, you can make your own style sheet, indicating the way you want to set headings. You and your secretary will then have a reference, and you will avoid switching styles halfway through a report. For a very long report, you may choose to indicate the level of heading by a circled A, B, or C in the margin next to each head. The typist can then refer to a key on the style sheet. This system is especially valuable if you use a word-processing pool. The format that follows is widely used for long reports in both industry and government.

Report Format

CHAPTER TITLES
   Chapter titles are set in all caps and centered on the page.

Section Headings

   Section headings are also centered. They are upper case and lower case and underlined. If your argument is logical, you should have at least two heads at every level of subdivision.

Section Subheadings
   Underlined subheadings, flush left, head each subdivision.

   • If you are going to divide a subsection
      further, you may do so by using bullets or some
      similar mark of distinction. These sections
      should be indented.

   —This level of subdivision should be further
      indented. It probably would not be used in a
      report written in paragraph form. If you are
      down to this level of division, think about
      whether the point is really significant.

In a report that does not have chapters, you may begin with centered, underlined headings (the second level above). In a memo or short report, this level, too, is usually eliminated. A memo of three pages or fewer usually begins with lower case, flush-left headings because a short memo rarely includes so much detail that it will need more than two levels of generalization (subheads and bullets).

Since chapter titles and section headings are broad in nature, some explanatory or introductory text should intervene between each of these and the next level of subdivision. The text should provide an overview of the major topic to be considered in the section, suggest what is to follow, and define any difficult or controversial terms. In the example about relocating the small-parts plant, a section might begin this way:

Location C Minimizes Capital Expenditures

Construction costs constitute 50 percent of the cost of moving our small-parts assembly. In several of the potential sites the costs of construction are lower than the $2 million estimated at Location C. However, the availability of industrial development bonds and municipal power must be considered in calculating actual capital expenditures.

Municipality Will Issue Industrial Development Bonds

Mayor Whiffen assures us the municipal government will issue bonds . . .

We do not recommend the use of Roman numerals, capital letters, and Arabic numerals to mark divisions, because readers may react to them by stopping to enumerate the thoughts that preceded. Unless your organization dictates this policy, we suggest you use numbers only if you want to emphasize a particular number of items and have indicated the total number in advance.

Making It Attractive

Pages of unbroken text are stultifying. They encourage the reader to allow his or her thoughts to wander. You may break up the page by inserting headings or by putting some of the information in tables and charts, although you won't let undue concern for aesthetics drive you to emphasize minor points or distort the argument.

Because stylistic devices help focus the reader's attention and send messages about you, it is important to give careful thought to their use. You can check your success immediately by looking at reports critically and by reading through the headings and emphasized points. Is each page attractive? Do the headings tell the story? Do the main points the reader should remember stand out from the body of the text?

Review some of your reports and memos. Would you add bullets, underlining, or capitals for emphasis? Is the presentation style consistent? Would you change any of the headings? Read something you are writing now. Can you improve it by emphasizing major points? By adding headings?

Constructing Visuals—Tables and Charts

Visuals (which in managerial reports are commonly called exhibits) are an essential part of any long and many short reports. Designing them is part of your job as a report writer. Many management writers construct tables or charts (including graphs) as part of the problem solving process; they find it helps them discover important relationships or significant trends they might otherwise overlook. Even if they don't use them as a problem solving tool, though, experienced report writers make rough exhibits before they write the first draft. Constructing charts and tables at this stage allows you to check the conclusions—the relationship on which you based a part of your argument may appear minor or even vanish when you work up the exhibit.

Before you begin to design your exhibits, take a little time to examine your resources. Your corporation may have a design department that's available for work on important communications. If you work for a large corporation, you should also check with the data processing department. If computer programs that generate graphs and flow charts are available, you may be able to save time and increase accuracy by having some exhibits done this way. If you can't get anyone to help you, local art stores can provide some of the materials you need. Many companies now produce sheets of dry transfer type in a wide variety of tones and textures for shading on graphs or special effects with symbols, letters, and borders.

Whether you construct your own exhibits or have help, you are responsible for the finished product. To make the most effective use of exhibits you should:

- Use them intelligently
- Select the appropriate form
- Tell the reader why each exhibit is important
- Keep it simple
- Make sure the exhibit is self-contained but tie it to the text
- Check to make sure it's not misleading
- Evaluate the completed product

Use Tables and Charts Intelligently

Management writers may be tempted to indulge in graphic over-kill for two reasons: they hope that attaching page upon page of exhibits will substitute for a well-thought-out and convincing argument; they have made a heavy investment of time and energy constructing visuals as part of the problem solving process and are reluctant to discard any of them. Force yourself to cut your losses if you find yourself in either of these situations. Like the stylistic devices discussed earlier, charts and tables are dramatic because they are visual. To include unnecessary exhibits devalues those that make the most important points. Once again, think of the needs of the reader and use only those graphic devices that:

- Display complex data simply and clearly
- Emphasize the important points in your argument

Always consider presenting material in tabular or graphic form if it will save your reader time and get your point across more effectively. How often have you received a report with a section of text that looked like this?

If you open a 2,000-square-foot store at Location A, hire a sales manager and three clerks for $34,000, pay the maximum annual rent of $10 per square foot and amortize preopening expenses of $15 a square foot over twenty years, assuming that 18 percent of net margin goes to variable operating expenses and that sales average $90 a square foot, at a 40 percent margin, pretax profits would be $3,000. However, your experience with small stores indicates that you can produce sales of $135 a square foot in such a store. In that case, you would have pretax earnings of $33,000. On the other hand, if you open a 4,000-square-foot store in Location B, where rent is $12 a square foot, you cannot expect to produce sales of more than $90 a square foot, which is the national average for stores of that size and which approximates what you sell in your present stores. In that location you would have one manager and five salespersons and pretax profits would be $14,000. I therefore recommend you open a 2,000-square-foot store.

The writer might have made it easier for the reader by presenting the same information this way:

I recommend that you open a 2,000-square-foot store in Location A. You can expect to achieve sales of $135 a square foot in that location based on your past experience; the likelihood of selling more than $90 a square foot in a 4,000-square-foot store is slim, given national averages and your record. Although some expenses would be proportionately less in the larger store, pretax earnings in Location A should be 2.4 times those in Location B (see exhibit 1).

Exhibit 1 may follow the page with the reference or it may be placed at the end of the report in a section labeled Exhibits. If exhibits are used with memos, they are usually placed at the end of the document. In this case the exhibit might look like table 8.1.

The table is far easier to understand than the paragraph littered with numbers, and it does a better job of showing the relationship between the two locations.

Using a graph not only condenses complex information, it also emphasizes important relationships. Forcing readers to determine the significance of a stream of undigested data makes them do your work for you and they may not draw the conclusion you want them to. What point was the writer trying to make in the following sentence?

Earnings over the past five years grew from $580,000 in 1970 to $710,000 in 1971 to $820,000 in 1972 to $960,000 in 1973 and reached $1,230,00 in 1974.

The writer might have made the point more effectively this way:

Earnings, which have doubled in the last five years, exceeded $1.2 million in 1974 (see exhibit 2 for five-year growth).

TABLE 8.1

Exhibit 1
Two-Thousand-Square-Foot Store Is Most Profitable

	Store Size	
	2,000 sq. ft.	4,000 sq. ft.
Sales	$135/sq. ft.	$90/sq. ft.
Total sales	$270,000	$360,000
Net margin (40% of sales)[1]	108,000	144,000
Variable operating expense[2]	19,000	26,000
Salaries[3]	34,000	52,000
Rent	20,000	48,000
Preopening expenses[4]	2,000	3,000
Pretax revenue	33,000	14,000

---

[1]40 percent is the average margin for all stores in the chain.
[2]Variable operating expenses average 18 percent of net margin through the chain.
[3]Salaries are based on this schedule: In a 2,000-square-foot store, $10,000 for manager; $8,000 for each of three clerks. In a 4,000-square-foot store, $12,000 for manager; $8,000 for each of five clerks.
[4]Preopening expenses are estimated at $15 per square foot amortized over twenty years.

Exhibit 2 might look like figure 8.1., shown on the following page. The reader now has no doubt about the main point the writer is making—that the $1.2 million is the culmination of five years of growth. Because readers remember images better than words, depicting relationships graphically helps them retain information. A reader will recall the plummeting line on a graph that shows the decline in a product's profitability far longer than he or she will remember the specific figures on which the graph was based. Therefore, exhibits, when used carefully, help the reader remember your argument.

Use an Appropriate Form

The decision about whether to use a table or a particular chart form depends on the material you're presenting.

Tables consolidate a great deal of quantitative data in a small space without losing any of the numbers themselves (as happens, for example, when you plot points on a graph). Although a table implies relationships, particularly growth or decline, it doesn't

Figure 8.1

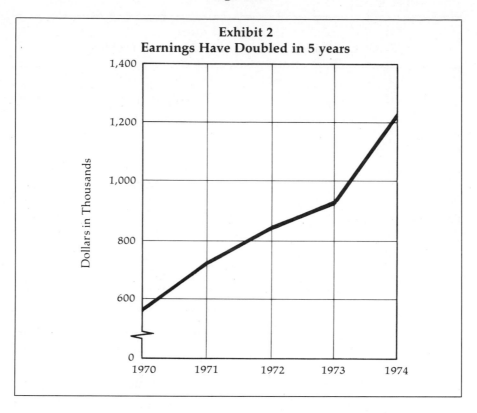

show those relationships. Therefore, tables are easier to misinter-
pret than charts. Note that table 8.2 is effective in delivering its
message because the relationship is fairly obvious—and it is reiter-
ated in the heading. If attendance had grown in some parks and
declined in others, a reader would have found it far more difficult
to grasp the point.

Even the most intelligent reader might miss the point of table
8.3. Why are the divisions put in this order? The list is neither in
alphabetical order nor ranked by sales volume. Probably the writer
simply chose to state the divisions in the order in which he or she
thought of them. And what is the significance of the information?
The reader cannot assimilate all the data; numbers are only useful
if the reader can see some relationships or change. The writer
might have made the table more useful by titling it "Two divisions

TABLE 8.2

Attendance In All Parks Has Grown Over Five Years
(In Thousands)

	1975	1976	1977	1978	1979
Allington Park	25	27	32	36	40
Pond Park	12	15	19	21	24
Freehold Pond Park	52	58	62	70	73
Samson Field	6	8	10	11	14
Center Field	12	18	22	23	26

TABLE 8.3

Sales By Division Since 1969
(In Thousands of Dollars)

	1969	1970	1971	1972	1973	1974	1975	1976
Watro	$24	$22	$31	$30	$44	$51	$60	$61
Ipsin	60	61	60	60	64	66	75	81
Caltran	22	29	30	33	32	34	45	36
Falvin	40	45	49	50	50	49	66	57
Sentex	17	22	23	25	28	40	60	60
Hapski	24	28	31	34	36	39	42	44

tripled sales since 1960" and by putting Watro and Sentex in bold-face type at the top of the list. But if the writer had been interested in showing the relative growth in sales among the divisions, this table would have been far less effective than a graph.

Charts show sophisticated relationships better than tables do. Since more than one kind of chart can indicate the same kind of relationship, you should choose the form that makes your point most effectively. The following guide and the illustrations on the next few pages may help you select the best one for your purpose.

Guide for Using Charts and Graphs

Message	Preferred Chart Form
Components of a whole	pie chart
Components of several wholes	bar chart
A ranking of items in one time period	bar chart
Comparison of several items in one time period	bar chart
Change over time of one or several variables	line graph
Comparison of change in several variables	dot chart

Look at some exhibits you have made recently. Did you choose the most effective kind of visual for each?

Figure 8.2 Pie Chart

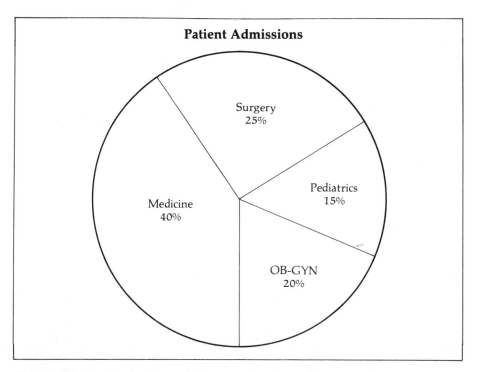

Patient Admissions

Surgery 25%

Pediatrics 15%

Medicine 40%

OB-GYN 20%

The pie chart shows parts of a whole, frequently in percentages. The individual figures must add up to the total, or 100 percent. Pie charts are often used to indicate proportions of budget spending or the composition of a substance or an organization.

Figure 8.3   Bar Chart

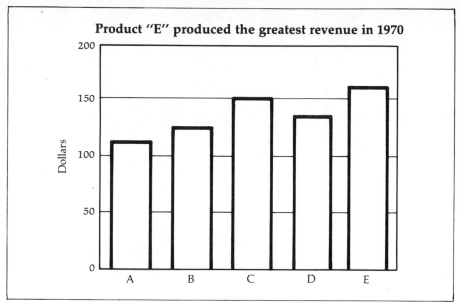

Product "E" produced the greatest revenue in 1970

Bar charts are particularly popular because they are simple to design and to read. They are used effectively to compare the size of several items at one time and to show the change in one item over time. (Bar charts may be vertical or horizontal. Vertical bar charts are frequently called column charts.)

Figure 8.4   Step Graph

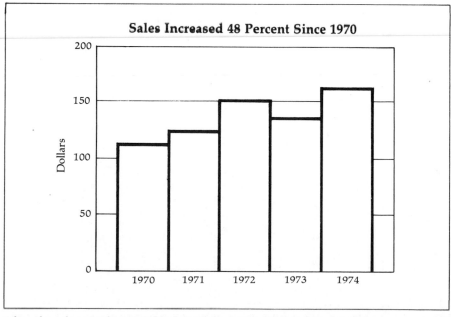

Sales Increased 48 Percent Since 1970

When the columns of a vertical bar chart are connected, the chart is called a step graph. It is used most frequently to show change over time.

Figure 8.5   Bar Chart Comparing Two Entities

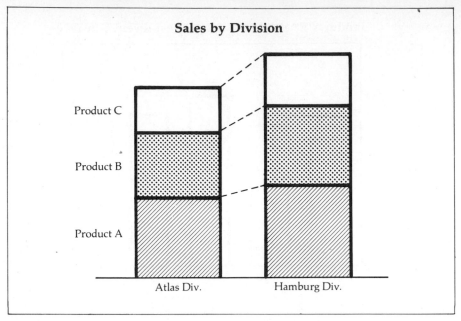

Sales by Division

Product C

Product B

Product A

Atlas Div.   Hamburg Div.

Bar charts are frequently subdivided to show change of a whole and its
parts or to compare several wholes and their parts.

Figure 8.6   Line Graph: Change Of One Item Over Time

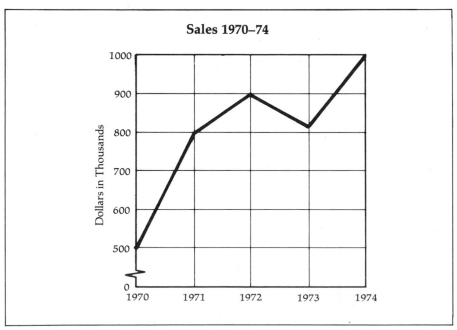

Sales 1970–74

Line graphs are the easiest kind of chart to produce accurately. With a piece
of graph paper and a pencil any report writer can make an effective one. A
line graph is used most frequently to show change over time.

Figure 8.7   Line Graph Showing Two Variables

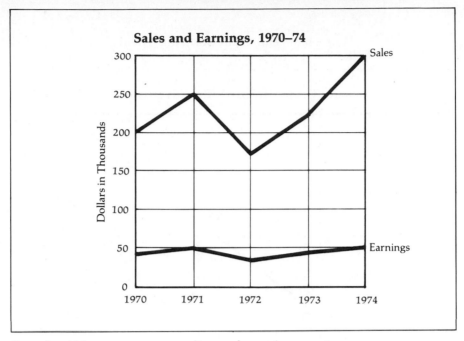

Several variables may appear on one line graph to make comparisons easy.
There should always be some relationship among all variables on one graph.

Figure 8.8   Surface Chart

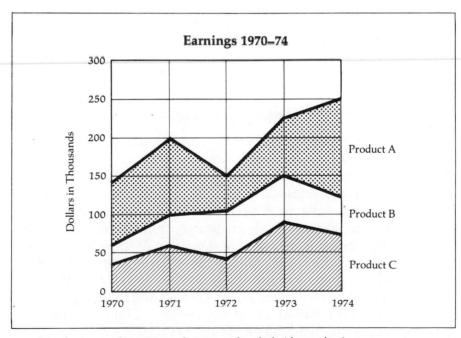

A surface chart is used to portray alteration of a whole (the top line) over
time and the relative changes among its components.

Figure 8.9   Dot Chart Showing Trend

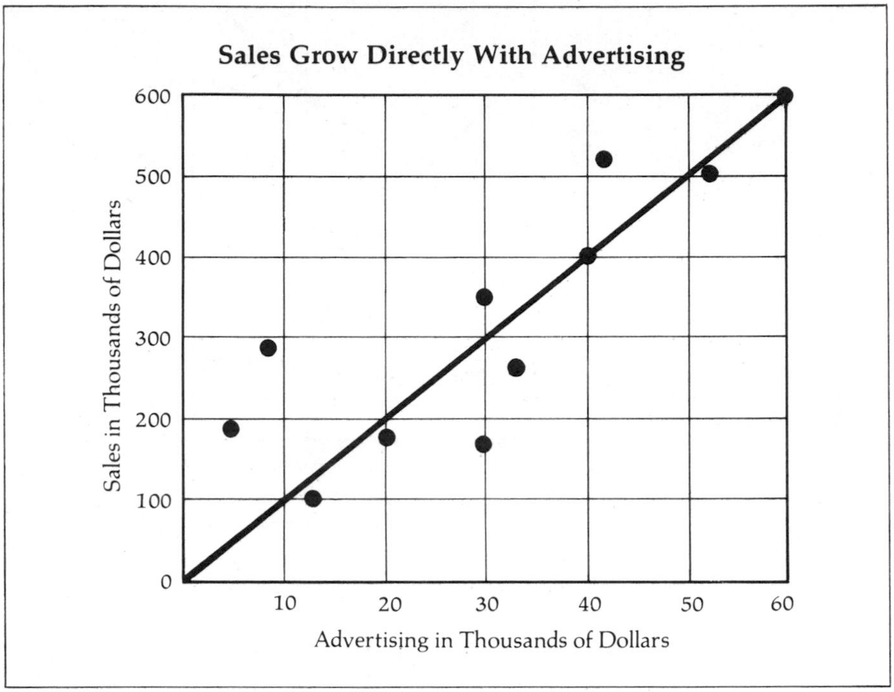

Sales Grow Directly With Advertising

The dot chart shows the relationship of one variable to another. A line is frequently used to indicate an expected pattern.

Tell the Reader Why the Chart Is Important

Look at the examples of different kinds of charts in this chapter. Although they all have headings, some of the headings are simple phrases referring to the chart's content; they tell the reader nothing about the chart's significance. Consequently, if the reader bothers to draw any conclusion at all, he or she may draw the wrong one. It is becoming increasingly customary in management, therefore, to write a heading as a simple statement of the relationship or trend you want the reader to remember from the exhibit. For example, look at the line graph labeled "Sales 1970–74" in figure 8.6. Why should a reader care about sales during this period? The writer might want the reader to remember the volume of sales. In that case, the chart should be titled:

Sales Topped $1 Million in 1974

On the other hand, if the creator of the chart wants to emphasize the fact that sales doubled, he or she might title it this way:

Sales Doubled Between 1970 and 1974

The title of a chart will reinforce your main point if you write it carefully.

Keep the Design Simple

Many newspapers, business magazines, and corporate publications are filled with glorious visuals, showing original combinations of the basic chart forms or using tiny figures of people, rows of machines, or piles of coins instead of the traditional bars on a graph. Unless you're exceptionally artistic, however, don't try to duplicate them. An overdecorated exhibit may distract or confuse the reader, and your goal is to communicate an idea. Make it attractive and neat but keep the design simple. Here are two points to remember.

Every Chart Should Make One Point Only. The first thing graphic designers try to determine when a manager gives them a rough chart is whether the writer is trying to tell more than one story. Frequently, their first step is to break such charts in two. If you have several things to compare (the performance of four or five divisions, for example) consider using a series of charts with a combined chart at the end.

Eliminate Any Information the Reader Doesn't Need. Round off any figures you can. For very large amounts eliminate the last three or six numbers and indicate the size of the reduction. (See figures and tables in this chapter for examples.) Streamline any table or chart to avoid unnecessary detail. If you're trying to show that total sales have increased 80 percent over the last five years, for example, don't break up sales by product just because you think the information is interesting. Such irrelevant information will only clutter up the exhibit, possibly causing the reader to lose sight of an important idea. The best way to avoid putting excess information on a chart or table is to write the heading for the exhibit, indicating its significance, before you prepare it. Then make certain that all information in the exhibit relates to that point alone. In figure 8.10, top of the next page, the maze of converging lines makes it difficult for a reader to determine the meaning of the graph. Which divisions are most important? What is the reason for comparing them?

Figure 8.10

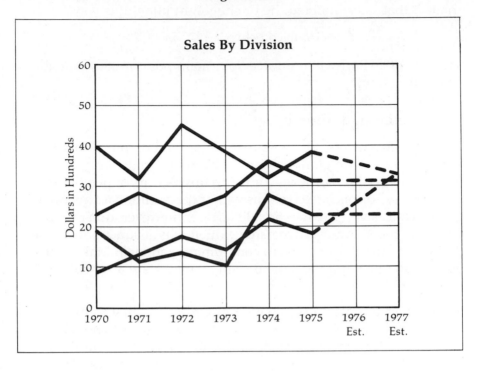

Make the Exhibit Self-contained but Tie It to the Text

A reader should be able to look at an exhibit and understand its
contents and significance without reading the text. Many executives flip through a report looking at exhibits, just as we all flip
through a good magazine looking at cartoons. A chart should
capture the reader's attention and transmit a message. If its heading indicates its significance, and if all of its parts are clearly labeled, the chart is self-explanatory. When you can, integrate tables
and charts into the text of a long report, locating them as close to
the place they are mentioned as possible; exhibits in an appendix
may never be seen. Regardless of where you put exhibits, however, you must refer to every chart or table in the memo or report
itself and, in order not to distract the reader, make your point in

the text. Do not force a reader to stop reading and look at the exhibit. It is far better to say, "Over 45 percent of our budget for fiscal year 1980 went for salaries, as indicated in exhibit 2," than "See exhibit 2 for budget figures." If you do not need a chart to amplify a point in the text, you should grit your teeth and eliminate the chart.

Make Sure Your Chart Is Not Misleading

Because visuals are so dramatic, they can exert a powerful influence in changing the reader's point of view. Since they represent a condensation of a relationship, however, they may also mislead by showing a distorted version of that relationship. According to one theory, for example, British foreign policy was influenced for many years by the fact that the British Foreign Office used only maps of the world that had been prepared on the basis of the Mercator projection, which shows countries nearer the poles as disproportionately larger than countries near the equator. As you prepare your exhibits (and look at charts prepared by others), be aware of their potential to deceive.

Be certain you use an appropriate scale. It's sometimes tempting to use a chart to exaggerate growth. The graphs in figures 8.11 and 8.12 were constructed on the basis of the same figures, but the graph in figure 8.11 suggests a much more rapid growth than that in figure 8.12 because the horizontal scale is collapsed. Look critically at any chart or graph to be sure that it is making a valid point.

If you are using two or more graphs to show comparison, be sure to keep the scale the same on both. The graphs in figures 8.13 and 8.14 are not comparable because the dollar amounts are not the same, but this is not immediately obvious to the casual reader.

If you are going to break columns to save space, you should do so at the bottom rather than the top of the chart. Any break should be the same for all items.

When an exhibit indicates change over time, the time should be indicated along the horizontal axis. Any number axis should begin with zero.

Indicate any external events that influence a comparison. A chart may be deceiving, even though the information and title are abso-

For comparison: scales must be the same

Figure 8.11

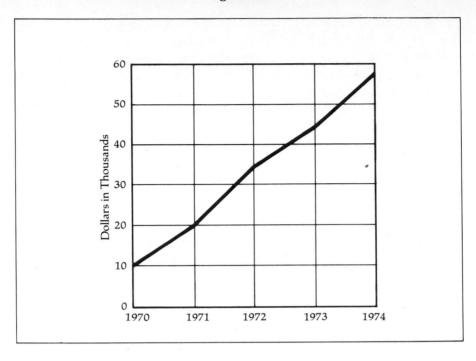

Figure 8.12

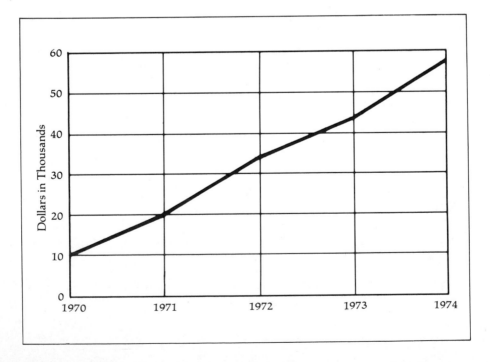

138

Figure 8.13

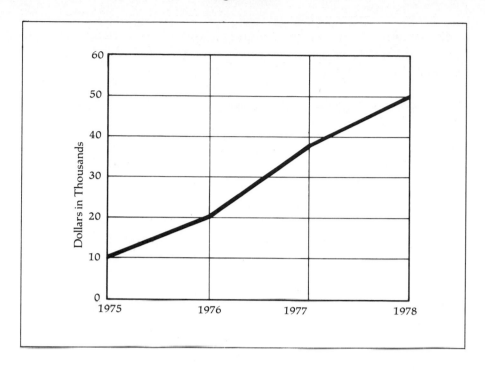

Figure 8.14

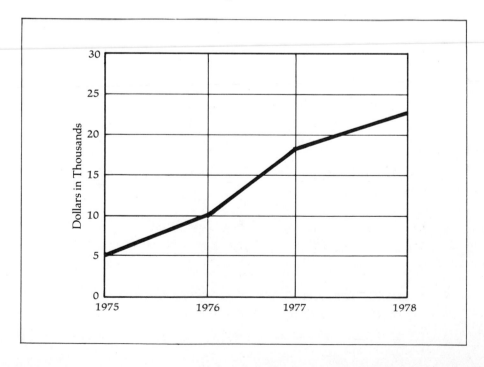

lutely accurate. If an external event influences one variable more than it does other variables, that fact should be noted on the chart, perhaps through the use of an arrow and a tag line.

Evaluate Your Tables and Charts

Once you've let your exhibits rest for a day or so, look at them without prejudice. The first thing to look for is whether you've succumbed to the temptation to overdo. One picture may be worth a thousand words, but a thousand pictures can be a crashing bore. Making thirty or forty charts for anything short of a major report may show lack of judgment.

You can also check your work by showing your visuals to co-workers who aren't familiar with the topic. Ask them if they understand what you are trying to say. Don't ask whether they like the exhibit, however. People feel free to comment on graphics. It's the classic case of "I don't know anything about art, but I know what I like." If you are offered suggestions about aesthetics, ask for the reasons behind the suggestions. Then decide for yourself. If your viewers don't understand the significance of an exhibit, however, you've got a legitimate concern.

Reviewing your exhibits using this checklist will help.

Exhibit Checklist

1. Does the exhibit clarify your argument for the reader?

2. Does the exhibit make one point, and one point only?

3. Does the title of the exhibit indicate its significance to the reader?

4. Does the exhibit accurately show relationships?

Review some of your recent exhibits by using this checklist. Would you change the exhibit or the title in any way?

SUMMARY

- The stylistic devices you choose to create an effective presentation should
  —focus the reader's attention on major points
  —guide the reader through the argument
  —make the document attractive
- Bullets, underlining, and capitals all emphasize major points; each has its own purpose
- In a long report, headings and subheadings are the best guides for the reader. They should
  —describe the material that follows
  —stand alone as an outline of the argument
  —be parallel in structure
  —follow a consistent format
- To check the logic of headings and emphasized points, read through them
- Exhibits are an important aid for the reader because they
  —save time
  —emphasize relationships
  —reinforce and dramatize major points
- Each kind of visual has characteristics that make it especially useful for conveying specific kinds of information. Always try to use the most effective form.
- Each visual should
  —have a title indicating its significance
  —be easy to understand by itself
  —be tied to the text

Case Study Exercises

1. **Complex.** Review your memo to senior management and put in any headings you feel would be useful. Emphasize the major points.

2. **Budget.** Review your memo to the investment committee. Add headings. What visuals would you want to include if you were Lerue making a presentation to the investment committee? How would you title each one?

Further References ————————————————

Brusaw, Charles, Alred, Gerald, and Oliu, Walter. *The Business Writer's Handbook.* New York: St. Martin's Press, 1976.
This basic reference book has an excellent section on graphs and tables with well-thought-out examples.

Ewing, David W. *Writing for Results.* 2d ed. New York: Wiley, 1979. Ewing's chapter 10 has a valuable discussion of graphs and tables.

9

REVISING IS
QUALITY CONTROL

Although deadline pressure may tempt you to skip the revision of your first draft, carefully revising your memo or report always pays off. This chapter will show you:

- How to revise for organization
- How to revise for language

Your secretary has just typed your first draft of a report on the implementation of a new training program for the keypunch department. You've spent hours on the thing—interviewing the keypunchers, talking with their supervisors, going over the background of training in that department, laboriously organizing the report—and you probably don't care if you ever see it again. You set a high value on your time, and revision may be one of the steps you can skip. Privately, you view it as sophisticated nit-picking anyway.

But absolute accuracy can only be achieved through carefully altering your prose to make it as clear and concise as possible. If a document is well organized and the language is correct, the reader will be less likely to misunderstand what you are trying to say, to be distracted (or offended) by flagrant errors, or to jump to the conclusion that because you are a sloppy writer you are also a sloppy thinker. Furthermore, even professional writers don't produce a perfect first draft—some of them revise as many as ten times. Except for long reports, you'll probably be able to schedule time for only one revision. But you can't delegate it. Although your secretary may be able to pick up some of your grammatical mistakes, he or she won't be able to spot most errors in meaning. And, although it's legitimate to give a draft of an important memo or report to someone else to read, people are usually reluctant to make comments on someone else's writing. In the end, you are responsible for what you write.

However, revision doesn't have to be a chore. Now that you've started to follow the steps to effective writing outlined in this book—solving the problem, developing a logical organization, and writing a first draft with a view to the reader's needs—you shouldn't have to do wholesale rewriting, throwing out whole sections and starting from scratch. In fact, you should spend less time revising than you did in the past.

Furthermore, revising is rewarding. When you revise, you can make something obviously better with a few minor changes—tightening up sentences by removing vague or unnecessary words, putting a topic sentence at the beginning of the paragraph, making sure that there are appropriate references to exhibits, and correcting headings. And you can spot unnecessary or redundant sections and delete them. In addition, as you begin to learn what sorts of errors you make most often, your first drafts will improve immensely.

Before you begin to revise, let the first draft rest for at least a day—if you're under deadline pressure, overnight will do. If you start to revise immediately after you finish the first draft, you'll be far too committed to what you've been slaving over to revise objectively. Building enough time for revision into your writing schedule will allow you to set a draft aside with a clear conscience.

Revision is a two-step process—reviewing for structural faults and correcting language. The first step is by far the most important. Frequently, if you can find and fix organizational flaws, problems of language and style disappear automatically. For example, convoluted sentences may well disappear when you tighten up the structure.

Revising for Organization

To be a conscientious editor, you have to put yourself in the reader's place. Intelligent readers are responsive. They question as they read. Although you have already checked the organization when you reviewed your diagram for problems before you wrote the first draft, asking yourself the following questions will give you a final chance to see things from the reader's point of view.

Does the structure jump out at you? Read through the whole document quickly. Can you instantly tell what the main point is? Is it easy to see what the main supporting points are? If you can't find them, knowing everything you know, chances are the reader won't be able to either.

Is the purpose clear? What significance does the main point have for the reader? Does the introduction tell the reader what the memo or report is about, why it is important, and how you will develop the idea? Is it clear what action should be taken on the basis of this piece of writing?

Is the organization logical? Check your contents page (in a long report) or your section headings (in a short memo or report) against your original diagram. Do all points at the same level of importance carry the same weight in the finished document? Does the finished document include all the points you made in the diagram? Check your headings: Do all the headings in the same style (all caps, for example) convey the same sorts of ideas?

Are the key paragraphs well organized? Is the first paragraph in each section a mini-introduction, answering the *What, Why Significant,* and *How* questions for that section? Remember that the heading is not part of the first paragraph. Many writers open the paragraph that follows a heading with a pronoun that refers to a noun in the heading:

Municipality Will Issue Bonds

They can be a primary source of funds for renovation projects in our region . . .

Because readers do not see the head as part of the text, such vague references will confuse them. Such faults are simple to fix.

Municipality Will Issue Bonds

Tax-free bonds are a primary source of funds for renovation projects in our region . . .

Also check the last paragraph in each section. Does it summarize the material in that section or lead the reader into the next section?

Are Your Transitions Accurate? Transitions reveal the relationships among your ideas. Transitions may be words, sentences, or whole paragraphs (in a long report). Make sure they are clear and valid. If you are constructing a deductive argument, for example, you'll want to alert the reader that you are drawing a conclusion by using such words as *therefore, thus,* and *accordingly.* If you are piling up assertions or evidence for your argument, you'll use terms like *in addition, similarly,* and *likewise.* If you are indicating a shift of direction, you'll want to pull the reader up short with *however* or *nevertheless.* Make sure, when you use such words, that they signal a relationship that really exists. Dropping them in at random merely confuses the reader.

Similarly, using the word *this* alone to introduce a new section or paragraph does not provide the reader with enough information. To start out with "This proves beyond a shadow of a doubt . . . ," without saying what *this* refers to, will send the befuddled reader back to the preceding paragraph. You'll often find, when you force yourself to add a noun, such as "this *finding*" or "this *discussion*," that whatever it is did not prove anything at all.

Did You Keep the Reader Moving Forward? Try not to send the reader back to earlier material in the report with phrases like "as previously discussed." Similarly, avoid referring to material you will be discussing later in the argument or the reader may skip ahead to see what you are talking about. Naturally, in a long report, you'll include references to the body in the executive summary, and if you have exhibits they must be referred to in the text. But all material necessary to the argument itself should appear where it will do the most good.

As you check through a draft with an eye to organization, resist the temptation to tamper with the wording. If you see a howler of some kind and it's easy to change, by all means change it. If you will need to go to a thesaurus for a better word or to stop to rewrite a difficult sentence, circle the phrase and keep on going. Circling the offending word or phrase will prevent you from missing it the next time through. But revising for organization and revising for language are separate operations. If you start hacking into the prose while you are revising for organization, you'll never be able to see the forest for the trees.

Revising for Language

Once you've fixed any organizational flaws, you're ready to work on the language itself. Revising for language, grammar, and punctuation are crucial. It's necessary to choose your words carefully because they are your only tools for telling the reader precisely what you mean. A word that means one thing to you may have a totally different connotation for the reader. Legal cases, for example, have been lost because of varying interpretations of a simple word like *speedy*. Although choosing the wrong word seldom has such dire consequences in management, writing "as soon as possible" when you mean "Friday" can lead to trouble.

Punctuation and grammar are equally important because they tell the reader the relationships between words and phrases. If you forget a vital comma or use commas to string together several simple sentences, the reader may have trouble following your ideas and may even have to pause to take stock. Furthermore, inaccurate grammar and punctuation may mislead a reader. Consider the writer who suggested that his store modify its atmosphere "to attract middle-aged women, who are concerned about buying fashionable dresses at low prices." Maybe that's what he meant to say (the comma sets off the clause that follows it, indicating that all middle-aged women are concerned about buying fashionable dresses at low prices—something the reader may doubt). It's more likely, however, that he meant the store should try to attract a specific class of middle-aged women—those who are concerned about buying fashionable dresses at low prices. If that was his intention, he should not have placed a comma between *women* and *who*.

There are many good grammar reviews and style manuals, and anyone who writes should have one for reference. (See the list at the end of the chapter for suggestions.) It also helps to read aloud what you have written. If you find yourself out of breath, as if you've just run the New York Marathon, you probably need to break up overlong sentences or insert sensible punctuation to provide legitimate pauses. In addition, you'll find that you can actually "hear" many awkward and poorly constructed phrases.

To make your writing immediately clearer and more understandable, you should keep in mind a few simple rules as you review your draft for language:

- Use language assertively
- Construct sentences to show relationships
- Say what you mean
- Choose words that work for you
- Use an appropriate tone
- Avoid sexist language

Use Language Assertively

Having confidence in what you are writing and stating it without reservation is as important as satisfying the needs of the reader. In any informal exchange, assertiveness means stating what you want to have happen and why. Just as some people avoid the first person through a mistaken sense that introducing themselves into the written document is somehow impolite or not sufficiently objective, others sprinkle their sentences with qualifying words or phrases like *apparently, in my opinion, it appears, it may.* As a college student dealing with broad topics about which you knew little, you may have gotten into the habit of including such phrases. But as a manager, you should have confidence in what you are saying: you cannot expect your reader to be persuaded by what you write if you hedge everything you say.

Use the active voice whenever appropriate. To refresh your memory about the difference between the active and passive voice, look at this example:

    ACTIVE VOICE: Grand Diamond opened a branch store.
    PASSIVE VOICE: A branch store was opened by Grand Diamond.

Compare the two. The active version is shorter and it's clear at the very beginning who is doing what to whom. Organization in sentences is similar to organization in paragraphs and whole reports—tell the reader the most important thing first. In sentences, it's usually most important to find out first who or what is doing something. Compare these two versions of the same sentence:

    WEAK: Some confusion is suggested by the data with respect to
            consumer preference.
    BETTER: The data suggest some confusion concerning consumer
              preference.

Some people in business and government argue that the passive is more polite and more dignified than the active voice. This rationale often simply provides an excuse for obscuring their real meaning or hedging their bets:

    WEAK: Sales volume for this year will be lower than previously
            anticipated.
    BETTER: Our department anticipated that sales volume this year
              would be 25 percent higher than now appears likely.

It's better not to conceal the truth, even if it's unpleasant. In the first place, using the passive to shield the person or department that took the action won't fool anyone. In the second place, telling the reader what actually happened positively and assertively will lead him or her to have confidence in you. It is, however, legitimate to use the passive when:
- The thing or person receiving the action is vastly more important than the person or thing performing the action

    EXAMPLE: President Kennedy was assassinated.

- The person or thing performing the action is unknown

    EXAMPLE: The letter was written anonymously.

- You don't want to cause unnecessary unpleasantness

    EXAMPLE: The Cleveland Index has disappeared from the library.
                (*Instead of:* Someone has stolen the Cleveland Index.)

Use action verbs. Forms of the verb *to be (is, are, was)* describe the existence of something. Action verbs describe something that is happening; they give a sense of movement to your writing. In addition, sentences containing action verbs use fewer words than other sentences. Many management writers, perhaps because they lack confidence in their ability to use words that are slightly out of the ordinary, fall back on forms of the verb *to be* or make nouns out of perfectly adequate action verbs. As you edit, you can correct for this habit and give your writing much more vigor in the process.

- Change forms of the verb *to be* to action verbs

    WEAK: There is a feeling among the marketing staff that . . .
    BETTER: The marketing staff believes that . . .

- Change nouns made from verbs back into verbs whenever possible

    WEAK: Marlin's survey established a preference of managers for
             dealing with a single vendor.
    BETTER: Marlin's survey established that managers prefer to deal
             with a single vendor.

Construct Sentences to Show Relationships

Writing sentences to show relationships among ideas will dramatically improve the clarity of your writing. Not only does a string of simple sentences make readers catatonic, it gives them no clue as to how the sentences relate to each other. If you don't construct your sentences to create such clues, readers will have difficulty understanding what you're trying to say. Look at this short example:

> The report is well written and concise. It provides a penetrating analysis of the personnel problems that resulted when the staff was reduced by 40 percent over a six-month period. This report will serve managers as a guide. It shows precisely what happened during the six months of the study. The writers challenge the usual view of the corporation's human resources department.

How do the thoughts expressed by each sentence relate to each other? There's no way a reader can tell without stopping to think, which forces the reader to do the writer's work. On careful examination, you can see that the first two sentences relate to each other because they both say something about the characteristics of the report. You might combine them this way:

> The report, which is well written and concise, carefully analyzes the personnel problems that resulted . . .

In this case, you've subordinated the description of the report's style to the idea that it carefully analyzes something. The reader now knows that you consider the report's content more important than its style—a helpful clue. The third and fourth sentences can also be combined in a way that shows their relationship to each other:

> This report will provide managers with a valuable guide because it explains events in detail.

The sentence now shows that the value of the report lies in its detailed explanation. As you revise, try to show relationships this way. You might try rewriting sentences several different ways to get a feel for what's possible. If it's appropriate, connecting simple sentences with a coordinating conjunction (*and* or *but*) is better than leaving them to stand alone, but your writing will be much livelier if you try to use such words as *because, since,* and *although* to alert the reader to relationships among your thoughts.

Combining sentences can be carried too far, of course. Some writers overload their sentences with too many ideas:

> Depending on the number and frequency of employees hired, a regularly scheduled training program might be feasible and allow for a more efficient entry process.

The writer obviously was trying to cut down on the length of the sentence, but obscured its meaning in the process. Part of the problem is the passive voice, but this sentence can be fixed easily by making it into two sentences:

> Depending on the number of employees we hire, we should consider a regularly scheduled training program. This program would contribute to a more efficient entry process.

Mastering parallel structure also shows relationships and improves the clarity of your writing. Parts of a sentence that are parallel in meaning should be parallel in structure. Parallel structure is obligatory when you are dealing with a series of items or actions, because the reader expects that you will demonstrate, by the way you structure the series, that the items are the same. Look at this example:

AWKWARD: The Division has no sales force, no experience in this type of marketing, and is not ready to make its move at this time.

IMPROVED: The Division has no sales force, lacks experience . . . , and is not ready . . .
[Each item in the series starts with a verb.]

You should take special care to use parallelism in lists broken out from the text because mistakes in such lists are painfully obvious.

WRONG: Our product has the following superior qualities:
1. Low cost
2. Multiple uses
3. Our product has potential for acceptance among the most market segments.

IMPROVED: Our product has the following superior qualities:
1. Low cost
2. Multiple uses
3. Potential for acceptance . . .

OR: Our product has the following superior qualities:
1. Its cost is low.
2. It has multiple uses.
3. It should be accepted by most market segments.

Say What You Mean

Anyone you write to is busy and harassed. If you pile on unnecessary words, phrases, sentences, and paragraphs, the reader will rightly resent your failure to serve his or her needs. Furthermore, your most significant points will be lost in the cloud of words. Saying what you mean economically requires you to eliminate excess words and avoid redundancy (repeating ideas unnecessarily).

Eliminate excess words. Most first drafts contain padding. It may be your habit to begin sentences with excess baggage like "the fact that" or "it's possible to conclude that," or "it is my sincere belief that." Writing assertively sometimes eliminates such phrases. Many excess words disappear when you convert verbs to the active voice. You can eliminate others by using verbs instead of phrases to describe verbs:

> WEAK: The fact that Ms. Burne is assuming the post of director of operations gratifies me.
> BETTER: I'm delighted that Ms. Burne will become our director of operations.

> WEAK: It is recommended that this survey be completed four months prior to the shipment of your new equipment.
> BETTER: We recommend that you complete the survey four months before we ship your equipment.

> WEAK: Those managers who were insecure tended to call fewer meetings than those who were competent.
> BETTER: Insecure managers called fewer meetings than competent managers.

Some overblown sentences, of course, must be totally rewritten:

> WEAK: We believe that a strategy of concentrating on the "mature shopper" segment represents the most viable choice.
> BETTER: Our company should concentrate on the "mature shopper."

> WEAK: As per your request to seek a reasonable solution to the problem in the redevelopment project, I would like to offer the following solution to the problem:
> BETTER: I suggest we solve the redevelopment-project problem by . . .

Watch out for long strings of unnecessary phrases. Spying these little baggage trains moving slowly through your paragraphs is a sure sign that cutting will improve the pace of your prose—and the reader's understanding.

> WEAK: Provision was made *for* the imposition *of* criminal penalties *on* those willfully neglecting their duties *under* the Act. [*This fault often accompanies use of the passive. This sentence contains four prepositional phrases—the reader can't grasp the point till he or she comes to the end of the string.*]

> BETTER: Under this Act, those who willfully neglected their duties
> were subject to criminal penalties. [*Reduces the prepositions
> to one in the main clause.*]

Avoid Redundancies. Sometimes repetition is necessary for clarity
or emphasis; usually it is a sign of sloppiness or insecurity. Eliminate words that, though different, mean the same thing.

> WEAK: You must realize that there is an *established* committee *al-
> ready in place.*
> BETTER: You must realize that a committee already exists. [*Remem-
> ber, there is no one right way to say anything. Your task is to
> find the words that come closest to what you want to say.*]

See how concisely you can write this paragraph without losing
any of its meaning:

> First, the set percentage rate of increase for the health care industry
> allows a rewarding of institutional inefficiency for those less produc-
> tive hospitals that have historically operated with a large margin of
> unwarranted costs. Conversely, those well-managed, efficiently uti-
> lized hospitals that have reviewed all areas of operations by depart-
> ment, determined levels of service, and reduced costs appropriately,
> will be penalized for operating on a narrower margin.

Maybe you came up with something like this:

> The set percentage rate of increase for the health care industry rewards
> inefficiency. Less productive hospitals will benefit; well-managed hos-
> pitals will be penalized.

You've cut the passage by more than one-half without losing
anything essential to the meaning.

Choose words that work for you

In most cases there is one word that conveys your meaning most
precisely. Frequently, that word is not a multisyllabic monster with
a Latin root, but a short word of Anglo-Saxon descent. As you
edit, you should be alert to any inaccurate or inexact words that
crept in as you were writing.

Watch for slipshod usage. Sloppy usage can embarrass you. All
the following examples are taken from real memos and reports.

EXAMPLE: Some attention should be given to the size of the room where the processing unit will be located, relative to the heat output and comfort of the operator. [*The* heat output . . . of the operator? *We've all heard of body heat but . . .*]

EXAMPLE: Management will be satiated by this alternative. [*Not unless it was a longer lunch than usual—the writer means "satisfied."*]

EXAMPLE: The marketing director isolated specific segments of shoppers. [*Not unless he or she goes in for vivisection. Segments are part of a whole.*]

EXAMPLE: The staff should be bipartisan and sexually mixed. [*Are we talking about androgynes? How about:* The composition of the staff should meet affirmative action standards?]

Avoid jargon, vogue words, and journalese. The meanings of some words are clear only to a specialized audience. You must explain them to anyone else. Other words are overused or misused. A few candidates for immediate banishment, unless used in their original sense, are *factor, dimensions, parameters* (of a problem), *interface, impact* (as a verb), *input, options, extrapolate,* and *utilize. Prioritize* and other nonwords may someday become accepted English terms, but until they are you should avoid them as well.

Journalese (sometimes called "elegant variation") shows disrespect for a reader's intelligence. Words like *garner* are seldom seen unless someone gets a sudden urge to liven up his or her prose or has recently been locked in a room with a five-year-old copy of *Time.* Avoid any word you would not use in everyday speech.

Use an Appropriate Tone

Natural writing is effective writing, and readers should be able to see the person behind the printed page. But writers frequently forget that what seems natural to them may be offensive to someone else. Consider your reader's preferences and biases and your own position within the organizational hierarchy to decide whether you should lean toward formality or camaraderie.

Humor is a special case because taste in humor is highly individual. What's hilarious to you may not be even mildly funny to someone else. In addition, humor doesn't travel well. (Have you ever tried retelling a joke you heard on television?) If your communication is passed along, the third person down the line may not know enough about the context to understand the joke, let alone find it amusing. Finally, humor implies that you have a special relationship with the person you are writing to—superiors may consider it presumptuous. It's safer to leave it out if you have any question.

No one wants to be offensive, but even innocent comments are easily misunderstood. An interviewer who compliments a female applicant on her attractiveness may find that she feels he is not treating her professional skills with the respect they deserve. In the same way, people who use ethnic slang and tell ethnic jokes about their own group may be deeply hurt if someone of another ethnic background makes the same jokes. Although humor is sometimes acceptable, discriminatory language and ethnic jokes are not.

Avoid Sexist Language

Sexist language attracts attention these days. Unfortunately, there are no pat solutions, and many recent proposals have outraged language purists. Thoughts traditionally expressed by the third person singular (*his* or *hers, him* or *her*) or substitutes for nouns incorporating *man* or *men* (like *mankind*) present special problems. The following recommendations can help you write memos and reports that are both non-sexist and clear.

Good solutions. Whenever possible, specify the person you are discussing. If you say Jim Hammock, everyone knows to whom the *he* or *him* in succeeding sentences refers. Use the plural *(they, their,* and *them)*. Instead of saying "everyone should listen to his subordinates," say "managers should listen to their subordinates." When giving examples, use *she* instead of *he* some of the time. Writing "the executive vice-president" followed by *she* will become easier with practice and may delight your readers. Consistently referring to judges and other power figures as *he* and to subordinates like keypunch operators as *she* is distasteful.

An acceptable solution. If none of the good solutions is appropriate, it is most useful to say *he or she,* or *she or he* when that can be done comfortably. But don't overdo it. It is ludicrous to write something like this:

He or she is responsible for making his or her own appointments, so give him or her the program schedule.

You might rewrite the sentence this way:

Each participant is responsible for his or her appointments and should be given the program schedule.

Nonsensical solutions. Using *(s)he, s/he* or *she/he* to avoid the awkwardness of *he or she* does nothing about *her or him* or *hers or his*. In addition, this unpronounceable phrase confuses readers who silently say words as they read. Alternating *he* and *she* (and other forms of the pronoun) is nonsense. Consider this example:

Everyone should study his manual daily. It could make a significant difference to her later on.

Three sentences later, the poor reader is totally confused.

When all else fails, some people use *he* to refer to both sexes. This traditional practice, however, is increasingly likely to irritate both men and women. If you decide to use *he* in the generic sense, you should state your intention to do so when you first use the pronoun.

Whatever form you choose, you should base your decision on both consideration for the reader's sensitivity and concern for the flow of the language. Any usage that jars or confuses the reader lessens the likelihood that your argument will be thoroughly read, understood, or accepted.

"Male" words and other indiscretions. Without getting into a discussion of such absurdities as renaming manhole covers, we suggest that every writer must be aware of the hidden, and often not so hidden, meanings of some words. Some common terms are demeaning. Secretaries are not *girls,* nor are all working females who are past puberty *working girls*. A man who is employed in a stockroom is a *stockclerk,* not a *stockboy.*

Many words that include the generic *man* can comfortably be changed without changing the meaning: *manmade* can be *synthetic, spokesman* can be *representative, workman* can be *worker,* and so forth. Many words, such as *chairperson,* which still sounds strange to some ears, are becoming increasingly acceptable.

Similar qualities in women and men are often described quite differently. A man is called "forthright"; a woman who acts the same way may be called "abrasive." Slanting your language in this way causes the reader to question your objectivity.

Miss, Mrs., Ms. Again, these salutations are a matter of preference. Some women return mail that is addressed to them as Ms. On the other hand, if you don't know whether a woman is married or single, it is probably safest to address her as *Ms.* If you are writing a letter to someone whom you have met or have spoken with on the phone, ask what form she prefers. Concern for the reader's sensitivity should be the guide.

Since revision is extremely important and rewarding, you should now try your hand at it. Pick a recent memo that didn't satisfy you (or, if you have not followed the case study exercises, choose one of the first drafts in Appendix 2) and revise it, asking yourself the questions in the chapter summary.

Sample Revised Memo

Delete titles — these men are on a first-name basis. See chapter 2.

To: Hank Berra, ~~President~~

Date: May 29, 1981

From: Sidney Wheaton, ~~Vice president for Personnel~~

Re: Proposed Managerial Training Program

Don't hedge — see chapter 9.

In the past our company ~~appears to~~ has

~~have~~ focused almost exclusively on

training programs for clerical and

technical personnel. Because of our re-

cent acquisitions, however, (positions)

Be specific — see chapter 9.

the number of ~~at the~~ managerial ~~level~~ have increased

35 percent. ~~greatly~~ Many of these positions are

filled by people new to management—

systems engineers from DPI, for exam-

Eliminate excess words — see chapter 9.

ple~~, which creates an immediate need~~
~~for managerial training programs. In~~

"And" is inappropriate; the expansion *caused* the demands — see chapter 9.

Because   has placed
~~view of~~ our expansion ~~and the~~ growing
          demands   these new
~~responsibilities being placed~~ on ~~our~~

managers, we must reassess our training

programs.

Change passive to active — see chapter 9.

I recommend
A two-part program ~~is recommended~~

Redundant

an
• Creation of ~~a skills~~ assessment

center to diagnose the skills and

requirements of new managers and to

identify high-caliber recruits.

Parallel structure — see chapter 9.

ion of leadership and communications
• Institut a six-month ~~training~~ pro-

gram for all new managers.

Less is more — see chapter 9.

~~This program will stress leadership~~
~~and communications skills.~~ This program

More logical order — see chapter 4.

will require a staff of six—two coun-
and
selors for the assessment center, three

trainers, ~~and~~ a director. Total cost

Refer to exhibits in text — see chapter 8.

will be $135,000. (See attached budget.)

New conclusion encourages action—see chapter 6.

I look forward to meeting with you
to discuss this program in detail.
Could we set up a 45-minute
meeting for the morning of July 2?

Proofread Your Memo or Report

Editing your first draft doesn't guarantee that your changes will be made. Typists are human, and you may have given ambiguous directions (typically, people forget to cross out all the words they replace when they make corrections). For anything important, proofreading the final copy carefully is essential. Even minor typos can be embarrassing; some are unintentionally humorous or offensive. Here are some suggestions if you're working alone:

- Don't be afraid to look up a word or phrase in a dictionary or usage book if it "looks funny." You'll often find you were right in the first place—but you'll never catch mistakes if you don't look for them.
- If you find a mistake in a sentence, correct it and then read the sentence again. It's easy to concentrate so hard on the first mistake that you miss an error a few words farther on.
- If a paragraph or section has numerous errors or extensive rewriting, read it aloud from beginning to end. If you're working quickly, you may omit words or forget to delete phrases you've changed. Reading aloud will help you find these slips.

For something that's extremely important, read the entire memo or report aloud to someone—spelling out uncommon words and inserting punctuation.

It's tempting to try to delegate proofreading to your secretary or simply ignore it altogether. But you, the writer, are ultimately responsible for the accuracy of the final document. Don't let all your work preparing and writing a report or memo be marred by carelessness at this stage.

Proofreading Marks

Although you aren't a professional proofreader, using standard proofreader's marks will help your secretary when you are revising and proofreading.

Mark	Meaning
⌔	Delete, omit word.
⌣	Close up.
#	Leave space.
¶	New paragraph.
No ¶	No paragraph.

Symbol	Meaning
→or ⌒	Run on. Connects words when space has been left or you have crossed out several lines of text.
(More) ↗	Rest of paragraph continues on next page.
⌐⌐	Center.
⊔⊓	Transpose letters or words.
(10)	Spell out, don't abbreviate.
let it stand	Let it stand (when copy appears to be deleted but you want it to remain).
¢	Lowercase capital letter.
c̲̲	Capitalize lowercase letter.
⋏	Insert comma.
⋎	Insert apostrophe (or single quotation mark).
⋎ ⋎	Insert quotation marks.
⋎	Insert semicolon.
⋎	Insert colon.
⋎	Insert hyphen.
⊙	Insert period.
productivity	Make all capitals.

SUMMARY

Revising for organization and language requires reading your report or memo at least twice, asking these questions:
- Is the purpose of the document clear within the first few sentences?
- Does the introduction cause the reader to ask the question I want asked?

- Do I answer that question?
- Is the logical structure of the report or memo clear from reading the table of contents or the headings?
- Are the key paragraphs well organized?
- Is the language forceful? Active verbs? Tight sentences? Precise words? No extra words?
- Is the tone acceptable? Have I avoided sexist language?

Case Study Exercise

Revise, for organization and language, the memo you wrote for the **Complex** case or the **Budget** case, asking yourself the questions in the chapter summary.

Further References

Many fine books emphasize precise use of language; three of the best are:

Bernstein, Theodore M. *Watch Your Language.* New York: Atheneum, 1976.
———. *The Careful Writer: A Modern Guide to English Usage.* New York: Atheneum, 1977.
Newman, Edwin. *Strictly Speaking.* New York: Warner Books, 1975.

For a good reference book on style, try either of these two:

Jordan, Lewis, ed. *The New York Times Manual of Style and Usage.* New York: Quadrangle, 1956.

A Manual of Style. Chicago: The University of Chicago Press, 1969.

For a short guide to style and usage, try either of these:

Kolb, Harold H., Jr. *A Writer's Guide: The Essential Points.* New York: Harcourt Brace Jovanovich, 1980.

Strunk, W. and White, E. B. *The Elements of Style.* New York: Macmillan, 1978.

10
HELPING OTHERS WRITE EFFECTIVELY

Learning to evaluate someone else's writing also helps you become a better writer. This chapter will show you:

- How to appraise writing tactfully
- How to review the writing of your peers and subordinates
- How to review and edit for superiors

It's 4:30 on a Wednesday afternoon. Last Thursday you asked one of your department heads to give you a report on the proposed reorganization of her department by Monday. You'll be using it as part of the monthly report to senior management due this Friday. She just handed you the report with numerous excuses about not having time enough to do proper research, and you're almost afraid to look at it. Hoping you won't be disappointed this time, you start turning the pages. With a growing sense of panic, you realize the report is disorganized, wordy, flippant—there's no way you can submit it without extensive revision. Disgusted, you cancel your earlier plans to go out to dinner with a friend and resign yourself to spending the night whipping the report into shape. You can't afford to be embarrassed by submitting it the way it is.

You should never get to this point. It's true that you frequently have to rely on the work of others when you write lengthy reports, and just as often you may have someone write a memo or letter to go out over your signature. But those writers will be less likely to let you down at the last minute if you help them learn to write more effectively.

Learning to evaluate someone else's writing also helps you become a better writer. As you develop your evaluative skills, you will become more aware of the different ways people express themselves, and learning to "read" people through their writing will help you communicate with them more easily. In addition, by casting yourself in the role of reader instead of writer you will become more sensitive to the needs of a reading audience. Appraising someone else's writing also sharpens your analytical tools so that you can see your own errors more readily. It's easier, after all, to see someone else's deficiencies than to see your own.

Learning to give effective feedback will benefit everyone involved. If you can offer a sensible evaluation of someone else's writing, you and that person will develop a mutual understanding about language and organization—which will in turn decrease the need for further review. Slips in communication skills tend to be incremental. Calling a person on an inaccuracy of grammar or organization the tenth time he or she repeats it is far more difficult than pointing out an error the first or second time: don't put off the inevitable. Although managers are sometimes reluctant to offer suggestions—evaluating any aspect of performance may make both the evaluator and the person being evaluated defensive—mutual confidence depends on effective feedback.

Before you call someone in to discuss his or her work or edit something for a superior, you'll need to appraise the writing itself. Following the guidelines below should help you.

Guidelines for Appraising Writing

Agree on limits. You may choose to appraise someone else's writing by evaluating, editing, or revising it. Your decision will depend on the nature of the request, if any, and on your relationship with the writer. But be sure to establish, in advance, whether what is required is written or oral comment, minor editing of the original document, or major revision. If you come to agreement on the extent of the appraisal first, you'll avoid the time-consuming game of sending something back, only to have it returned with all your changes ignored.

Find the thesis. Always read a document completely before you pick up a pencil. Your goal is to scout out the main points and the thesis statement or conclusion. That thesis statement, the main point of the piece, is usually in the first paragraph in short memos. The writer gets high marks if it is easily found and is clearly stated.

Look at the support. Think about the opening statement. Is it clear what the problem is, why it is important and how the author will develop his or her argument? That is, if the thesis statement is "I recommend we hire Joe McDonald as executive vice-president," you assume that the support will march along in the form of reasons. If the thesis statement describes or defines a problem, you may expect the rest of the piece to categorize or classify the problem that is being discussed. The thesis statement "McDonald Motors has several severe problems" is probably the prelude to a discussion of the major problems McDonald Motors has. Does the author keep his or her implied promise in supporting the thesis statement?

Outline the argument. Flip through the comunication and find the supporting points for the writer's argument. These may well be the topic sentences of the paragraphs in a short memo or the lead sentences of the first paragraphs in each section of a long report. Are these the points you expected the writer to make? Do they adequately support the argument or round out the description? If the argument is complex, outline it on a separate piece of paper. Are the sections parallel? Is the argument ordered logically?

Use a checklist. Use a checklist like the one at the end of this chapter to organize your thoughts so that you can give useful reactions.

Edit cautiously. If you must write on the manuscript itself, do so in light pencil and try not to make dictatorial comments. Remember that every black mark will remind a writer of unpleasantries in the past—an English teacher, perhaps, who used to proclaim "the pen is mightier than the sword," while obviously wishing for a sword. Resist the urge to use two or three heavy lines to delete a sentence—no one likes to see his words blotted out as if they were an offense to human decency. Avoid exclamation points. If you want to suggest improvements, do so by bracketing the words or phrases that might be left out or changed. Then write your suggestion above. Don't defeat your purpose by writing contemptuous phrases like "Awkward" or "Meaning?" in the margin. Try to recommend a few changes in the wording instead.

Even if you were asked to edit, do not change someone else's words without a good reason. The urge to see your own words in print is enormous. One editor we know keeps this motto prominently displayed: "The strongest drive is not love or hate. It is one person's need to change another's copy." Be wary of this tendency. When in doubt, always query the writer rather than change the words yourself.

Focus on structure. It is often possible to correct grammar or usage errors by changing the structure of the document. Although many people resist suggestions about grammar or usage on the ill-founded theory that you are inflicting your stylistic whims on them, they may be willing to consider structural changes. It is often easier to demonstrate that a change will make the argument easier to understand than to state flatly that the prose is ungrammatical. For example, someone who splits infinitives thoughtlessly may be persuaded to use another verb form on the principle that the substitute form is stronger.

Be tactful. If the writer has asked you for written comments, try to start with the large issues and work down to the details. Always remember to phrase criticism as gently as possible. Writing anxiety does exist, as surely as math anxiety does, and harsh criticism may guarantee that the writer will never ask for another evaluation.

Reviewing for Peers and Subordinates

Whatever you were asked to do about someone else's writing, try to talk to the writer about ways of improving rather than returning something with written comments. If your goal is to improve the quality of your staff's writing, meet with each person and share your thoughts about writing habits and practices. Try to schedule the meeting just before giving a writing assignment. This meeting may provide staff members with their only opportunity to learn just what you expect in the way of written communication. They cannot, after all, read your mind; and they may be reluctant to ask questions for fear of seeming ignorant.

Giving Feedback on Drafts

Once you have met with a staff member and discussed precisely what you want, you should provide an immediate opportunity to put the discussion into practice. Try to make the first assignment after your meeting relatively short. The shorter the piece, the fewer problems there are likely to be, and the better chance you will have to avoid defensiveness. You should ask to see a draft rather than a final memo or report. A draft, by definition, is unfinished. Completed memos or reports inevitably contain tiny shavings of the writer's ego—perhaps only a phrase or word he or she thought was especially appropriate, perhaps the entire structure of the argument. If you question such things in a completed document, you may find that you've stepped on a land mine—the offended writer may refuse to accept anything further you have to say.

When you meet with the writer to discuss the draft, keep criticism tactful and constructive. It's not enough to simply "dislike" the way a person writes. You must be able to make concrete suggestions about ways to improve. If you have isolated several problems, offer only a few suggestions at a time, usually beginning with suggestions about improving structure. Sometimes simply asking for a shorter version will eliminate a writer's affection for redundancy. Usually, comparing the shorter and longer versions will show the writer that writing can be improved dramatically.

Staff members are also more likely to adopt your suggestions if you can honestly say that you have found certain techniques helpful yourself. You might, for example, mention that you always write an executive summary before you write the first draft of anything dealing with a complicated or technical topic. Or you might show the staff member a diagram you developed for something you have written recently. Show someone a report you wrote that went through several revisions to demonstrate that you don't get these things right the first time either. Make it clear that writing is hard work for you, too, but that you have found improving your skills rewarding—and be specific about the rewards.

Strategies for Giving Feedback on Completed Memos and Reports

Sometimes, of course, you won't be able to comment on a memo or report in draft form. By far the best way to give feedback on a final version is to let the piece of writing or the writer provide it for you. If the letter, memo, or report has only minor problems, you can pass it along as is and let the writer take responsibility for it. For example, if you are submitting someone's report as part of your own report, you can make sure that the writer sees the recipient's comments on it. Similarly, if you have a staff member write a letter for you, you might consider letting the writer see the response to the letter, which may demonstrate that the letter didn't communicate as well as it might have. At this point, the staff member may initiate a discussion on ways to improve—the best way for such discussions to start.

If something written for you has serious problems, however, merely passing it along will backfire. You'll be guilty of bad judgment and you'll have to take responsibility for making the writer vulnerable, not an ideal way to establish trust. If serious problems exist, see if you can make it easy for the writer to provide his or her own feedback by asking some nonthreatening questions such as, "How do you feel about this memo or report?" Usually, writers are well aware when they've written something that doesn't make sense, and they'll start a discussion of the gaps or faults themselves. If that doesn't happen, you can try being more specific, by saying, for example: "I'm having trouble understanding exactly what you're saying in this section. Do you think you could explain it to me?" Generally, once the writer starts to explain, he or she will see that there's a communication problem and may even suggest ways to fix it.

Even if the memo or report is totally unacceptable, remember that you aren't doing the writer a favor if you take it upon yourself to rewrite it. A poor writer cannot be expected to learn anything if you do the rewriting. You'll only get another poor piece of writing the next time you give him or her an assignment. Furthermore, doing wholesale rewriting yourself will damage your relationship with the writer—you'll be resentful because of the extra work you had to do and the writer will be angry when he or she finds out about it.

Involving Your Staff Makes Writing More Effective

Whenever possible, involve your staff when you set deadlines for any important project. Writing always takes substantially longer than you believe it will, and setting arbitrary deadlines without consulting your staff members will cause them untold frustration. Don't dash off a memo saying, "I need a report on the Spider account by September 8." First think about precisely what information you need to take action. Write it down. Then call the staff member in and say something like, "Morris, I need a report on the activity in the Spider account quickly, because the marketing manager will be out in Omaha during September and he'll need to know about any complaints. When can you get the report to me?" If Morris says he can get it to you by September 15, ask him if there is any other work he can delay so that he can get it to you more quickly. Taking his workload into account this way makes it more likely that the memo will come in when you want it.

For complicated reports involving several people, you should negotiate the deadline and scope of the project at the beginning to get the most realistic deployment of personnel. You may be requesting something that simply cannot be achieved in the time you set. Make sure that the people involved establish practical intermediate deadlines for the completion of research, outline, executive summary, appendixes and exhibits, first draft, and final copy. Furthermore, although delegation saves you time, it's a good idea to sign off on the outline of the report before the actual writing begins. Catching gross errors of focus and organization at this point will help insure that the final product is acceptable.

Let the people you work with know that you are willing to accept their suggestions about improving your own writing skills. Someone may have been secretly covering for you by correcting simple grammatical mistakes or by adding phrases to clarify your meaning. Encourage your secretary to question anything that does not seem clear. You need this sort of commentary to keep yourself honest. You should also consult with your staff. Ask them if you could change your writing habits in any way that would help them do their jobs more effectively. Ask them if there are any routine writing tasks that you should delegate. Not only will this provide you with valuable information, but asking for suggestions always makes it easier for others to accept your recommendations for improvement.

Progress should be recognized. Once you have given concrete suggestions for improvement, keep track of what your staff members are doing. People are far more motivated by praise than by criticism. For example, when a staff member has cut down the average length of his memos by one-third, with a corresponding increase in clarity, be sure to tell him or her that you are very pleased by this improvement. At the same time, be certain all staff members realize that improving written communications is a continuing process.

Reviewing for Superiors

If all senior executives could write meaningful, well-organized prose, members of their staffs would find life easier. Unfortunately, many senior executives need help with their writing. As you become known as an effective writer, your advice may well be sought by others. You may be called upon to review external as well as internal communications. Editing the writing of superiors is emotionally more difficult than evaluating for peers or subordinates. If you're editing for superiors, be pragmatic. Change obvious errors of grammar and usage if you can cite a rule to support your version; leave intact anything you can without losing your self-respect; question anything you are uncertain about. (Of course, you will not question something you can easily check yourself.) Be sensible. Remember that you don't know for sure what the author was thinking about. Changing "the effect is not unsubstantial" to "the effect is substantial," though it will make a shorter phrase, may alter the writer's meaning. If you can justify a change by claiming that a general reader will not understand what the writer has in mind, or if you can show that there is a grammatical error, the changes will probably be accepted gracefully.

Frequently people don't remember what they write, so you may, by returning clean copy instead of the edited version, have changes pass unnoticed. The writer may even take pride in the way "his" or "her" prose reads. But be certain, before you return a retyped version, that the writer approves of your doing so.

Checking Your Evaluation

Regardless of whether you are revising, editing, or evaluating for a peer, a subordinate, or a superior, success depends on being both flexible and positive. Read first for the structure of the argument, then for appropriateness of tone and language, and finally for overt errors. You can use the following checklist to review memos and reports written by yourself and others.

Writing Evaluation Checklist

1. Is it structurally sound?
   —is the thought logically developed?
   —do paragraphs and headings clearly reflect that development?
   —are there any constructions that don't make sense?
   —do the connecting phrases show correct relationships , between ideas?

2. Does it answer all the questions it raises?

3. Is it concise?
   —does it tell the reader the facts he or she needs to know and no more?
   —are all unnecessary words and phrases deleted?

4. Is it appropriate in tone and language?
   —is the tone appropriate for the reader to whom it is aimed?
   —is the language adaped to the vocabulary of the reader?
   —are all technical terms and abbreviations explained?
   —is the writing free of sexist words or phrases?

5. Are there errors of grammar, spelling, or punctuation?

6. Summary evaluation: Is the memo or report effective? (Use the scale below.)

       Superior   Acceptable   Unacceptable

SUMMARY

- Learning to appraise other people's writing helps
  —improve your writing
  —improve your staff members' communication skills
- Always read the document completely before commenting on errors of structure, grammar, language, and tone
- Use tact when appraising someone else's writing
- Choose the best method of giving feedback:
  —comment on drafts
  —let the writing or the writer provide feedback
- Be pragmatic when editing for superiors
- Use a checklist

APPENDIXES

How to Use the Case Studies

Reading a lot of words about writing is easy, but applying the ideas when you write yourself is more difficult. As a way to test your understanding of the material, and to try out new techniques, we suggest you do the exercises at the end of each chapter, beginning with chapter 2. These exercises are based on the two cases beginning on the next page. Doing them will let you work through the writing process for one problem from beginning to end and finish with a well-written, attractively presented memo.

The cases, which are similar to those used in many graduate schools of business administration and public policy, are based on the experiences of real people facing complicated problems. The Complex Assembly Corporation case presents an ethical problem; no numbers are involved. In the Budget Finance Corporation case you may base your answer on the bank's goals alone or you may use the financial data included in the case to support your decision. You may, in the Complex Assembly case, decide not to make a recommendation; in the Budget Finance case you are asked for one. We suggest you read both cases and choose the one that interests you most. If you are ambitious you may try your hand at both.

Because there are no "correct" answers in writing, Appendix 2 gives at least two approaches to each exercise. Comparing your responses to those of other managers confronted with the same problem is a valuable way of sharpening your skills.

1

CASE STUDIES

Complex Assembly Corporation

In late May 1977, John Russo, chief engineer at the Complex Assembly Corporation, sat at his desk shuffling through stacks of test results and notes and puffing on his pipe. Russo, who was sixty-two, had been with Complex for twenty-five years. He enjoyed his work and considered himself part of the Complex "family." Russo had planned carefully for his retirement at sixty-five, and in two years would make the final payment on a 42-foot boat, on which he planned to live. Now, if he did not approve the test results before him, he faced the possibility of early retirement.

The Company

Complex Assembly Corporation, with over $100 million in annual sales, was one of the largest U.S. manufacturers of specialty wheel assemblies for heavy machinery. Early in 1977, the company had won the contract to construct nose-wheel assemblies for 300 military aircraft that were being built by High Flying Aerospace Corporation. The contract was important to Complex for several reasons. To minimize the effects of the extreme cycles to which the heavy machinery business was prone, management had for some time been looking for applications of its technology to other industries. But the custom-design nature of its operation was not applicable to any of the mass production markets, and attempts to produce parts for the automobile industry had proved a costly error. In addition, in the early 1970s Complex had been unable to deliver on a contract with High Flying. After a four-month delay, High Flying had cancelled the contract. Not only had Complex lost the $100,000 it had invested in research, development, and testing, but the company had not been able to sell a wheel assembly to any major aircraft producer since.

In its attempt to win the High Flying contract at any cost, Complex had submitted a bid so low that management expected to lose money on the initial sale. However, since wheel assemblies are designed for specific aircraft, replacement parts must be bought from the orginal builder. Complex expected the initial loss to be minor compared to the income the company ultimately hoped to generate from the sale. Furthermore, if this contract went well senior management expected to earn several million dollars annually in additional sales to other aircraft firms within a few years. When the contract was signed, the division VP called together everyone who was to work on the project and explained its importance to the company. He emphasized the need to do a good job and to complete the work on time. Russo had been away on a special assignment during the development of the assembly, but one of the engineers told him that when the VP left, Glen McGoly, manager of the design engineering department, closed the meeting by saying, "Hundreds of jobs are on the line. This contract has to be successful—see to it that it is."

The light-weight wheel assembly that had won the contract for Complex was a new design. Its weight advantage was directly attributable to an innovative ball-bearing housing designed by one of Complex Assembly's most capable engineers, George Simpson. A lanky thirty-five-year-old, Simpson had come to Complex three years before. He was a loner and put in long hours. His work was careful and precise and his superiors recognized him as a "comer." While this was the first aircraft wheel assembly for which he had been solely responsible at Complex, he had previously worked for an aircraft manufacturer. Several other engineers had seen the housing plans and had questioned aspects of the design, but High Flying had approved the specifications.

As designer of the assembly, Simpson was named project engineer for its development. He, in turn, assigned Sam Pilawski to build the test model and to oversee the first tests. (See figure A.1.1 for Engineering Division reporting structure.) Pilawski, whose engineering degree was in aeronautical and astronautical science, was excited at this opportunity to take on such an important project.

Complex had just ten weeks in which to run the first tests and deliver the first 100 completed assemblies. Because time was a major consideration, the parts for the assemblies had been ordered in quantity before any tests were made. It was Pilawski's responsibility to

Figure A.1.1

Engineering Division Reporting Structure

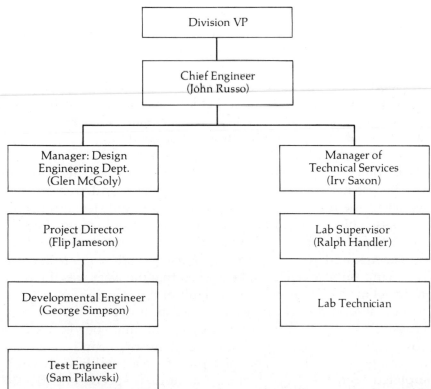

take the first parts that arrived and develop a prototype assembly that could be used for the initial qualification tests. He was also to oversee the production of the first fifty units from which ten would be chosen for further testing. Qualification tests for military aircraft are more extensive than for civilian planes, and High Flying had given Complex very specific and detailed test specifications. The tests fell into two categories, simulated tests at the plant and tests under actual flight conditions at High Flying.

The Tests

Simulated Tests:
- Prototype: 1,000 simulated stops at normal speeds with zero failures;
  100 simulated stops at high speeds with zero failures.
- Ten assemblies chosen at random from first fifty off the line:
  1,000 simulated stops at normal speeds with zero failures;
  100 simulated stops at high speeds with zero failures.

Flight Tests:
- Nine of the ten tested assemblies: 100 landings at normal speeds;
  50 landings at high speeds.

As soon as the first parts arrived, Pilawski built a prototype assembly and went directly to the test lab with it. The first 100 simulated landings at normal speeds were successful. He was delighted and left the laboratory to tell Simpson the good news.

Within two days the assembly had been subjected to 1,000 simulated landings at normal speeds and the high-speed tests began. Pilawski watched the first ten high-speed tests and was about to leave when the technician called him back. On the eleventh test the wheel assembly froze, causing the wheel to stop turning. Pilawski and the technician quickly dismantled the assembly and found that the bearings and the ball-bearing housing had worn irregularly. When Simpson was called in, he argued that the wear was the result of a defect in the bearings, not the fault of the housing.

It took several days to build a second prototype. This assembly successfully completed the 1,000 stops at normal speeds but froze on the eighty-fifth high-speed landing. Simpson again insisted that the bearings were at fault. The third prototype assembly successfully completed both the 1,000 landings at normal speeds and the 100 landings at high speeds. Curious, Pilawski dismantled the assembly and found that both the housing and the bearings had worn badly. He knew that this assembly could not have survived many additional landings. Although the prototype had passed the test, Pilawski was concerned about the wear on the bearings and the housing and went to Simpson. Simpson stuck to his original position. Noting that the assembly had satisfactorily passed the first portion of the laboratory tests, he demanded that Pilawski order the production of the fifty assemblies from which ten would be chosen at random for the second part of the test. Pilawski agreed to proceed. But he kept the worn housings and the bearings from the first tests in his office. Simpson kept the successful model and returned it to the lab.

Pilawski had ten days between the time he gave the OK for production and the completion of the fifty assemblies. During that period he repeatedly took out the worn ball-bearings and housings, looked at them, and replaced them in the cabinet. As soon as the random choice of ten assemblies was completed, in-plant tests began again. All ten assemblies successfully survived 1,000 simulated landings at normal speeds. But only five of the assemblies withstood the 100 landings at high speed. Pilawski went back to Simpson with the results. The five frozen assemblies had irregularly worn housings and bearings. Simpson demanded that the test be repeated. This time it took two weeks for the bearings to arrive, leaving Complex only four weeks before the promised delivery date. Six of the ten assemblies successfully survived a hundred landings at high speed. Meanwhile, Pilawski spent two days alone in his office, making his own computations based on the size, weight, and structure of the bearings and the housings. At the end of that period, he was convinced that the housing was simply too light to survive the stress of continual use. He went to Simpson with his figures. Simpson indignantly insisted, once again, that the problem was a defect in the ball-bearing. Since there were now eleven assemblies (five from the first test and six from the second) that had passed the simulated tests, Simpson demanded they select ten of these, and proceed to flight testing.

Convinced that even the successful assemblies would not survive the flight tests, Pilawski decided to go to Simpson's superior, the project's director, Flip Jameson. Jameson, known behind his back as "Flop," had come up the corporate ladder the hard way. Although he had begun work as a draftsman and had no engineering degree, he was in charge of all engineers working on projects slated for production. His position as the supervisor of men with academic credentials far more impressive than his own did not make him popular.

As project director, Jameson was responsible for getting the job done. He had assured High Flying several times that the assemblies had been tested, were successful, and were almost ready for delivery. Now, if he conceded that Simpson's design was not satisfactory, the project would not get out on time, if ever, and Jameson would be responsible to senior management for its failure. He tried to convince Pilawski that there really could be no problem; Simpson was an experienced engineer and obviously knew what he was doing.

Pilawski insisted that they could not send High Flying assemblies that had been selected from two groups of fifty. In frustration, Jameson agreed to one more run of simulated tests.

Simpson and Jameson hung over Pilawski as he prepared for the production of fifty new assemblies. Simpson personally selected each bearing that went into an assembly.

The simulated landing tests at normal speed were again successful. Simpson hung around the lab throughout the testing. On the afternoon the normal-speed tests were completed, he opened the assemblies, examined each of the bearing and housings, and replaced those that looked worn. Pilawski, who found him alone in the lab, objected. But Jameson was "out" and could not be reached; he was the only one with immediate authority to stop Simpson. Pilawski's next step was to approach Ralph Handler, the lab-test supervisor, who would be responsible for writing the test report.

"Look," said Pilawski, "this assembly just isn't going to make it. It's going out there on that airplane and it's going to freeze and everyone in the plane is going to be killed."

Handler was taken aback. "What does my technician say?"

"He hasn't been around when Simpson opens the assemblies. The first failures are in the log, of course, but they are all marked 'defective bearing.' He doesn't know about any of this. He is running another set of tests at the same time and he goes back and forth between the two."

Handler pondered the problem. His boss, Irv Saxon, had just had a severe heart attack and probably would not return to the job. McGoly, whose engineers used the technical services division, was taking over temporarily. Handler went to him for advice.

"It isn't so terrible, you know. We've never done anything like this here before, but it's done at other places," McGoly said. "These tests far exceed anything that a plane will normally go through. There simply isn't a chance anything will go wrong in real use. And we're really on the line with this one. If it is successful, there will be promotions here. If not, we may all be out of a job. Let's just get on with it. Time is short."

"What are you going to do about it?" Pilawski asked Handler after the meeting with McGoly.

"If they want a qualification report, I'll write one. But I have to tell it like it is," Handler said. "No false data or false reports are going to come out of this lab."

"Then how can you let Simpson run tests after he's fiddled with the bearings?"

"I'm not his boss," Handler retorted. "I only write reports, I don't run tests."

On the high-speed test, nine of the wheel assemblies survived 100 landings. On the evening before the tenth assembly was to be tested, Handler found Simpson checking the housings and bearings. Simpson said it was a routine check. The assembly passed the test.

"That's it," Simpson said. "Let's get going with that report."

"You know what that report's going to say," Handler reminded him. "I don't tell anything that isn't true."

"You don't have to," said Simpson. "You have ten assembly units that passed the test."

"But you tampered with one."

"I was only checking it out of curiosity. The log doesn't show any changes."

Handler realized that was true, since the log was kept by the technician. At that point McGoly entered the lab.

"Champagne for everyone. We've passed the test—Complex is on its way to the top again. Ralph, you'll have a division of your own soon."

Handler had taken the job at Complex in order to make his wife happy. She had not been well and had wanted to return to the town in which she had grown up, and to her parents. Complex was the only place in town where he could do the work for which he was trained. What would happen to his family if he refused to sign the report, he wondered.

Pilawski simply couldn't believe the whole thing. The test results, with Handler's signature and McGoly's approval, were on their way to Chief Engineer John Russo's desk before the assemblies went to High Flying for flight testing.

Pilawski decided he had to get to Russo before the test results did. He told Russo the whole story and showed him the original worn bearings and housings and his own and Simpson's calculations. Russo, who had extensive experience in wheel-assembly design, quickly saw the flaw in Simpson's calculations and the weaknesses in the housing. However, Russo also knew that the wheel assemblies were due at High Flying in two days for flight tests and that the first 100 production models were due in two weeks. He knew if they opened the ten assemblies going to High Flying, and changed any worn bearings and housings, there was virtually no chance that any of the assemblies would freeze during the test flights.

Russo thanked Pilawski for the information and said he'd get back to him. He then took his notes from the meeting and went across the hall to his good friend Susan Wish, a marketing expert who had "grown up" with Russo at Complex. He told Wish the story and the two considered the wheel-assembly calculations. Finally, Wish turned to Russo.

"Look John, you're sixty-two and you're going to retire in three years. You have a 40-foot boat waiting for you and you're anxious to take off for the Caribbean. What are the alternatives? We all know the tests on these assemblies far exceed anything that any plane normally experiences. All of the tests at normal speeds were satisfactory. It's really very unlikely that anything will ever go wrong. If the worn housing and bearings are replaced on the tested assemblies, the flight tests should go just fine. The top brass thinks that this contract is important and everyone along the line has approved the tests. If you don't sign, you're going to have to go out on a limb for your position. If you do that, and people go along with you, we will lose a contract and people here will lose jobs. If people don't go along with you, you'll have no choice but to resign. That plane probably won't be in use for a couple of years, anyway, and it's always possible that they'll alter the whole assembly before then."

John Russo returned to his desk. He had to decide what to do.

Budget Finance Corporation

On December 8, 1972, John Lerue sat in his office at a major New York bank holding company. At nine the next morning he was to meet with the corporation's investment committee to discuss a proposed $1.2 million loan to Budget Finance Corporation. He had not yet decided what to recommend to the committee or what data he wanted to present in the form of exhibits. He began, again, to review the proposal, both in terms of the bank's interests and Budget Finance's potential for success.

Finance Industry Note

Finance companies buy paper (accounts receivable) from retail firms and use that paper as collateral to secure loans from a factor or bank, using that money to buy more paper. A simple example should make the economics of the industry clear: Company A pays $75 for $100 worth of accounts receivable. It then takes the note for $100 to a factor or bank, and borrows $100 at 12 percent. Even if the factor or bank deducted the interest in advance, Company A would have $88, with which it could buy $117 worth of accounts receivable. In reality, the finance company deducts its interest in advance by purchasing accounts receivable at some percentage of face value, while the bank or factor generally collects interest over the period of the loan. Purchasers of the goods frequently default on payments. Thus, the percentage of face value that a finance company will pay for a note depends on the risk of default and the interest rate the bank or factor charges the finance company.

The Proposal

Early in 1972, Robert Ephram, president and principal owner of Budget Finance, had proposed to Lerue that the bank buy $1.2 million in convertible debenture bonds from his company. Budget was in the business of buying paper from small retailers who sold furniture and household goods in low-income neighborhoods in the greater New York area. Ephram believed he had developed a system that would increase the percentage of purchasers who actually made all payments under the terms of their credit agreements with the retailer. He argued that the bank should grant Budget the $1.2 million loan, both because it was a good business deal and because the loan was in line with the bank's commitment to support businesses in low-income neighborhoods.

The Bank's Commitment

The bank had substantial loans outstanding to small businesses in all parts of the city. Since late 1968, however, management had prided itself on making a high proportion of the bank's loans in low-income neighborhoods and advising small businessmen in these areas on financial matters. During late 1971 and early 1972 the bank had conducted a "Street Program," in which representatives of the bank—branch officers and public relations personnel—had gone into poor neighborhoods to explain banking and good business practices to groups in schools and to business associations. Senior management considered this effort good business as well as a civic duty, since it was anxious to protect the loans made in these neighborhoods. Bank advertising, in newspapers and on television, emphasized management's desire to help ghetto entrepreneurs.

Because the bonds that Ephram proposed that the bank buy could be converted into common stock, the bank might, at some future time, share in the ownership of the company.

The Budget System

When Ephram and Lerue first met, Ephram had outlined in detail his plan to decrease the percentage of defaults on loans in low-income areas. As he explained the problem, the prevailing financial arrangements reflected the retailers' lack of commitment to the customer. The retailers' principal interest was in delivering the merchandise and submitting the contract to a finance company. As most of the retailers dealt in only one product and repeat business was uncommon, there was little incentive to keep the customer happy. The moment the sale was concluded the retailers felt that their relationship with the customer was over. This attitude, according to Ephram, led retailers to adopt a number of questionable sales techniques that contributed to customers' unwillingness to pay for merchandise:

1. **Misleading promises**
   Salesmen, particularly those who sold merchandise door to door, often made unrealistic claims about the value of merchandise.
2. **Poor quality products**
   Many of the products sold by these companies were of poor quality, although prices were considerably higher than for equivalent or better products in a department store.

3. **Lack of service**
   Although salesmen and advertising literature extolled the virtues of follow-up service and repair facilities, these facilities were often inadequate to meet demand and frequently were located in places customers were not able to get to.

In addition, Ephram maintained that retailers did not actively seek down payments. As long as they could sell their paper at a reasonable discount to the finance company, down payments were relatively unimportant. Salesmen frequently contributed part of their sales commission to the down payment, making up their losses through increased sales volume. Ephram believed a customer who made no down payment had little or no commitment to ownership.

Ephram went on to claim that between 1968 and 1970 Budget had developed a system to counter these problems. The company:

1. Agreed to purchase all contracts from the retailers with whom it dealt.
2. Insisted on a minimum down payment of 20 percent for purchases made by a new customer.
3. Advanced the retailer only 50 percent of the total purchase price, holding the remainder in a special Dealer Reserve Account. The retailer was paid by Budget as payments were received from the customer.
4. Provided management, administrative, and accounting services to assist the retailer.
5. Provided merchandising assistance by arranging loans to help retailers broaden their product lines.
6. Established minimum standards of quality for merchandise sold by retailers with whom it worked.
7. Served customers through bilingual communications.
8. Represented the customer when he or she received faulty merchandise.

In the written proposal that Ephram had delivered to Lerue, he made the following claims about the unique qualities of Budget Finance:

1. **A Trained Management Team**
   Whereas most finance companies our size have three or four low-salaried employees, we have built up a management team that has had broad experience in all phases of our corporate activites. Members of the management team have backgrounds in finance, admin-

istration, and sales, gained both in small companies and in multinational organizations.

2. **Fully Computerized Operation**

   In our business it is essential to have absolute control over Accounts Receivable at all times to detect default trends by dealer. We have dedicated considerable time and money to developing computer programs that will track accounts by type of merchandise and location. The use of random access storage in the computer will vastly increase our control capabilities. It is our ultimate intent to receive daily management statements from our data processing center.

3. **Large Company Concept**

   Even though Budget Finance Corporation was family owned in its early years, we insisted on audited statements. We have legal advice from a major New York law firm. Personnel has been trained to absorb and handle additional responsibilities. Controls exist to verify and check the handling of incoming funds. All our thinking has been in terms of a large organization.

4. **Limited Delinquency Losses**

   Most finance companies do not withhold sufficient dealer reserves. For these companies, any losses beyond those expected represent direct operating losses. Under the Budget concept, the finance company is only affected adversely if the total losses exceed 30 percent of the paper purchased, because the dealer's reserve account is charged for bad debts. Thus, the downside factor is very limited.

5. **Established Retailer Responsibility**

   We finance the cost of merchandise for the retailer; his profits and overhead are obtained out of the collection of the accounts receivable. The retailer receives needed cash and the customer is served better because the vendor is committed to perform his part of the bargain until the last cent is collected.

6. **Specially Trained Personnel**

   Our personnel have been specially trained to handle the problems of minorities and economically deprived persons. We have hired persons of Hispanic descent and maintain close contact with retailers of Latin American origin. All our communications with the Spanish-speaking community are in Spanish and our Spanish dunning notices are not merely verbatim translations of our English notices, but are indeed "Spanish" notices.

In 1972, when Ephram came to Lerue with his proposal, the Budget Finance system had been in effect for two years and the company had approximately $2 million in receivables. Budget factored these receivables through a commercial corporation. Ephram was anxious to consolidate the company debt and build a line of bank credit, which would be less costly.

The Principals

Ephram's ability as a salesman impressed Lerue. He believed that Ephram's charm would attract retailers, who would prefer to deal with him rather than with smaller, less supportive credit agencies. In addition, Lerue believed owners of small businesses would be convinced by Ephram's arguments that they would actually make more under his system than by dealing with the standard loan companies. Ephram had ten years of experience in the finance business.

Ephram's partner, who had been born in Buenos Aires, had spent five years as a coffee futures broker and fifteen years as an accountant and banker. He understood the financial aspects of the business and served as a link to the Spanish-speaking community.

The National Economy

The year 1972 had been one of economic growth, and in December economists were optimistic about 1973 and the long run.

The *Business Week* that had arrived on Lerue's desk that morning included the following 1972 data:

Housing starts for November up 10 percent from November 1971

Personal income for November up 10.5 percent from November 1971

Wholesale and retail inventories for October up 6 percent from October 1971

Lerue made these predictions for 1973 based on the projections of a group of leading economists:

Real growth in GNP	5 percent
Price increases	4 percent
Average unemployment	5 percent

The stock market had broken 1,000 during October, and analysts on Wall Street concurred that business would be good and unemployment would not exceed 5 percent for at least two years. Lerue saw no reason to anticipate an economic decline over the short term.

Although there had been some talk among bankers during the past week that a credit crunch was possible within the next twelve months, his bank's senior economist had told Lerue that morning that he did not agree with those prognoses. The prime rate was 5.5 percent and he anticipated little increase.

New York Economy

New York had been slower to recover after the 1968–69 recession than had other parts of the country. Few of the ghetto areas of the Bronx had been rebuilt and large portions of the borough were, in Lerue's words, "a wasteland." The lack of economic growth in New York had been blamed, by many, on business's unwillingness to build in an area in which the skilled labor force was declining rapidly. The nonwhite population of the city continued to grow, and middle-class whites were moving to the suburbs in increasing numbers. Lerue had been responsible for loans to medium and small businesses in all five boroughs of New York and he knew the owners were barely breaking even. In spite of the optimistic projections for the nation, Lerue felt less sanguine about the economic future of New York.

Lerue agreed with Ephram's argument that the primary market for time-payment purchases in New York would continue to grow and he accepted Ephram's estimates that in 1972 the Budget "market" extended to 1.5 million buying units in New York and New Jersey and that each unit had an annual disposable income, for furniture and capital goods, of $400.

Of the many documents included with the proposal to the bank, Lerue was especially interested in the income and expense figures (see table A.1.1). As he considered what recommendation to make to the investment committee, he chose to view the conversion part of the proposal as attractive but unlikely. He did not believe the bank was interested in going into the finance business. He viewed the bonds as a straight 10 percent loan.

TABLE A.1.1
Budget Finance Corporation
Comparative Expense & Income Analysis

FORECAST, EXPENSES
Actual (1968/69–1971/72) Forecast (1973/77)
(in thousands of dollars)

	68/69	69/70	70/71	71/72	1973	1974	1975	1976	1977
Salary Expenses:	100.0	152.3	168.4	196.0	290.8	576.0	945.0	1353.0	1839.0
Office Expenses:									
Rent[1]	2.1	2.9	2.4	4.6	6.0	36.0	78.0	120.0	120.0
Telephone	11.8	21.6	20.3	16.6	25.9	56.0	96.0	150.0	226.0
IBM[2]					12.0	36.0	36.0	36.0	60.0
Office Supplies[3]	26.1	35.2	29.7	30.5	16.0	24.0	36.0	60.0	80.0
Depreciation	3.1	2.7	3.1	3.5	1.0	3.0	5.0	7.0	10.0
Miscellaneous	12.9	28.8	14.7	8.8	21.0	38.0	64.0	84.0	108.0
Office Expenses	. . . .	. . . .	. . . .	. . . .	5.0	8.0	9.0	9.0	11.0
SUBTOTAL	56.0	91.2	70.2	64.0	113.3	259.0	414.0	632.0	887.0
Administrative Expenses:									
Professional Fees	6.4	11.2	12.3	20.9	36.0	36.0	48.0	60.0	78.0
Travel/Enter-tainment[4]	10.1	10.8	10.0	15.6	22.5	54.0	84.0	108.0	162.0
Auto Expenses	6.2	2.7	3.1	4.8	8.0	24.0	24.0	24.0	24.0
Miscellaneous	0.7	1.7	1.3	0.1	12.0	24.0	24.0	36.0	48.0
SUBTOTAL	23.4	26.5	26.7	41.4	78.5	138.0	180.0	228.0	312.0
TOTAL EXPENSES	179.4	269.9	265.3	301.4	482.6	973.0	1539.0	2213.0	3038.0

FORECAST, INCOME
Comparative Income Analysis
(in thousands of dollars)

	68/69	69/70	70/71	71/72	1973	1974	1975	1976	1977
Interest & Disc. Earned[5]	385	589	484	430	409	1,817	3,792	7,018	11,008
Premium Income[6]	17	31	31	31	13	67	158	310	458
Charges to Dealers[7]	27	19	35	5	54	127	237	386	541
Other Income[8]	. . . .	. . . .	26	13	27	86	249	485	1,014
TOTAL INCOME	429	639	576	479	503	2,097	4,436	8,199	13,021

[1]The increase in rent beginning in 1974 is based on anticipated expansion needed to meet business growth.
[2]IBM charges beginning in 1973 and increasing in the next year are based on expansion of the data processing system.
[3]Includes stationery, postage, office supplies, and data processing (1968–72).
[4]The increase in travel and entertainment expenditures is based on the institution of management seminars and education programs for retailers and members of the Budget staff.
[5]Indicates the income from the loan of money to the purchaser; controlled by the usury laws of the states involved.
[6]Time payment arrangements include life insurance and accident and health insurance. A portion of the premiums of these policies is paid to Budget by the insurance company.
[7]The retailer is charged a $10 fee per contract for a credit check.
[8]These monies come from late charges and other services, such as accounts receivable management, outside consulting services, and specialized services like mailings and auditing, which the company provides for dealers.

2

SOLUTIONS TO CASE STUDY EXERCISES

This appendix contains several approaches to the Complex Assembly case questions and the Budget Finance case questions. All of the Complex Assembly answers appear first, chapter by chapter. When there are two responses, those marked "a" refer to a memo to the division vice-president, and those marked "b" refer to a memo to Pilawski. For the Budget Finance case, those responses marked "a" refer to a memo recommending making the loan, those marked "b" refer to a memo recommending against making the loan.

Complex Assembly Corporation

Chapter 2

a. Russo, whatever his decision, will have to notify his immediate superior, the division vice-president.

Reader Guideline

Subject of the report or memo: *Wheel assemblies for High Flying*

Name of the primary reader: *division vice-president*

Question the reader might ask: *What can we do to salvage the High Flying contract?*

My position in relation to the primary reader:

—professional: *I report to him.*

—personal: *none*

How extensive is his or her knowledge of the subject: (great, minimal, nonexistent—describe)   *Technical knowledge, but not as great as an engineer's*

What are his or her biases about the subject?   *Believes fulfillment of High Flying contract crucial to continued existence of Complex Assembly*

What are his or her significant managerial traits and stylistic preferences?   *Insists on short memos*

Who are the secondary readers?   *None*

Is anyone else likely to receive this report?   *Board of Directors, CEO*

---

b. Russo may also choose to notify Sam Pilawski of his decision.

Reader Guideline

Subject of the report or memo: *Action I will take on wheel assemblies*

Name of the primary reader: *Sam Pilawski*

Question the reader might ask: *What are you going to do about the contract?*

My position in relation to the primary reader:
—professional: *I'm several levels higher in the organization*
—personal: *remote*
How extensive is his or her knowledge of the subject: (great, minimal, nonexistent—describe) *Extensive knowledge, including proprietary information on testing failures*
What are his or her biases about the subject? *Believes assemblies were tampered with; believes defect will result in fatal crash*
What are his or her significant managerial traits and stylistic preferences? *Conscientious, stubborn*
Who are the secondary readers? *None*
Is anyone else likely to receive this report? *No*

Chapter 3

In analyzing the question "Should I accept the test results and send the assemblies?" Russo might choose to draw two analysis trees: one considering the possibilities if he sends the assemblies (figure A.2.1) and one considering the possibilities if he does not send them (figure A.2.2). Russo might select the following criteria against which to judge his alternatives.

Limit of Freedom	Reason
Not endanger human life	Ethical judgment

Negotiable Criteria: (ranked on a scale of 1–5 with 5 the most significant)

Criteria	Weight	Reason for Weight
Preserve image of reliability	5	All future contracts are dependent on maintaining a reputation for completing contracts close to schedule.
Avoid loss of High Flying contract	4	Loss of this contract will cost jobs and will hurt the company's image.
Not result in loss of my job	4	I need the remaining years of income to fulfill my retirement dream.
Not hurt Pilawski	2	He is a good engineer, but can get another job.

Figure A.2.1

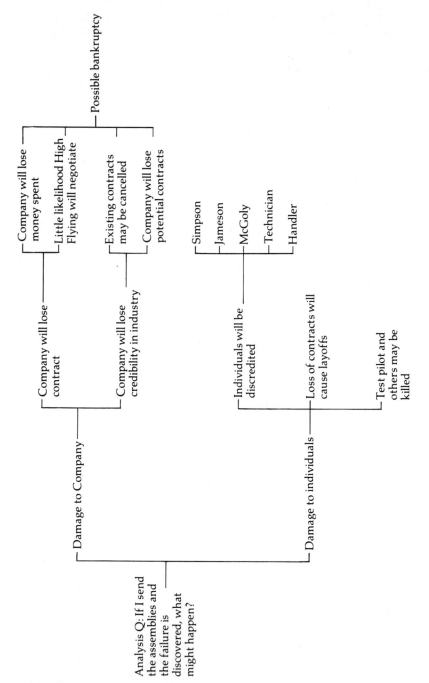

Figure A.2.2

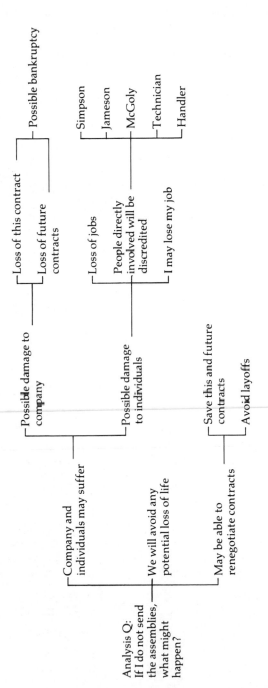

Russo might view the limit of freedom this way:

> Sending the assemblies would put a test pilot's life in jeopardy. Therefore we should admit to High Flying we have failed.

Or he might view it this way:

> The chance that a life will be lost is nil. Therefore I can consider the alternatives in terms of the negotiable criteria.

a. He might then continue this way:

Alternative: Send the parts

	Value	(X Criteria Weight)	Reason
Preserve image of reliability (5)	2	10	I believe the news of the test failure will ultimately get out.
Avoid loss of High Flying contract (4)	3	12	We can probably get away with this long enough to reconstruct the faulty part.
Not lose my job (4)	4	16	Time is on my side.
Not hurt Pilawski (2)	0	0	No chance of convincing him.
Total score		38	

Alternative: Don't send the parts

	Value	(X Criteria Weight)	Reason
Preserve image of reliability (5)	5	25	News of the failure will ultimately get out.
Avoid loss of High Flying contract (4)	0	0	If we don't send parts, we will lose contract.
Not lose my job (4)	0	0	Top management is dedicated to the success of this product.
Not hurt Pilawski (2)	5	10	He will be delighted.
Total Score		35	

b. Or this way:

Alternative: Send the parts

	Value	(X Criteria Weight)	Reason
Preserve image of reliability (5)	0	0	We will be found out.
Avoid loss of High Flying contract (4)	4	16	We will complete contract and make changes that will avoid suit.
Not lose my job (4)	4	16	I can convince management I wasn't responsible.
Not hurt Pilawski (2)	0	0	He will not understand.
Total score		32	

Alternative: Don't send the parts

	Value	(X Criteria Weight)	Reason
Preserve image of reliability (5)	3	15	Should be able to convince industry our rejection shows reliability.
Avoid loss of High Flying contract (4)	1	4	Unlikely we can renegotiate.
Not lose my job (4)	4	16	I think I can convince them I wasn't responsible.
Not hurt Pilawski (2)	2	4	He will be delighted, but will suffer personally.
Total score		39	

Chapter 4

a. Russo might decide to tell the vice-president about the test results and recommend that the company send the assembly as is. He might then group his assertions this way:

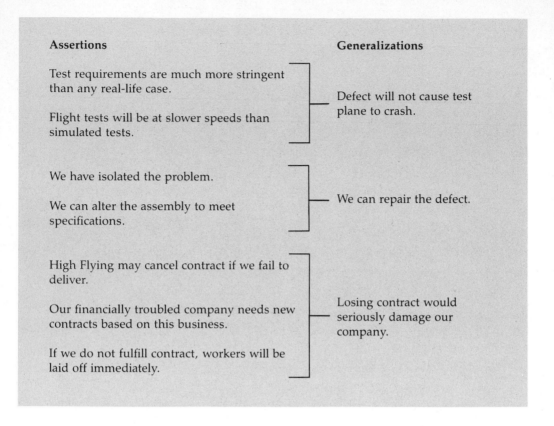

Assertions

Test requirements are much more stringent than any real-life case.

Flight tests will be at slower speeds than simulated tests.

We have isolated the problem.

We can alter the assembly to meet specifications.

High Flying may cancel contract if we fail to deliver.

Our financially troubled company needs new contracts based on this business.

If we do not fulfill contract, workers will be laid off immediately.

Generalizations

Defect will not cause test plane to crash.

We can repair the defect.

Losing contract would seriously damage our company.

In a memo to the vice-president, Russo might decide to order his assertions inductively to support his contention that Complex should send the assemblies to High Flying. He might choose an order based on the two criteria he will discuss, beginning with the limit of freedom:

1. Defect will not cause plane to crash.
2. Loss of contract would seriously damage our corporate image.

Taking the needs of the vice-president into account, he will omit both his personal criterion, that any delay in sending the assemblies on will destroy his retirement dream, and his concern about Pilawski.

b. If Russo decides not to recommend sending the assemblies, he might choose to explain to Pilawski the consequences of his decision. He could group his ideas this way:

Assertions	Generalizations
Pilawski will be seen as an informer. Co-workers will shun him.	Pilawski will suffer personal losses.
We will lose High Flying contract. We may lose future contracts.	Failure to complete contract will cause loss of business.
Some jobs will be lost as a result of cutbacks. Some heads will roll.	Failure to complete contract will cause people to lose jobs.

If Russo decides to tell Pilawski the problems Pilawski may face, he may do it in a deductively ordered memo in which the order is

Major Premise:	People who reveal problems are blamed for them.
Minor Premise:	Pilawski is calling attention to a situation that will result in loss of business and jobs.
Conclusion:	Pilawski will be blamed for the loss of business and may suffer personally.

Chapter 5

a. Figure A.2.3 shows Russo's organization tree for his memo to the division vice-president.

b. Figure A.2.4 shows Russo's pyramid diagram for his memo to Pilawski.

Note that, in both examples, as Russo moves from grouping to ordering to drawing a diagram of his memo, he is refining his argument.

Chapter 6

a. Russo might begin a memo recommending sending the assemblies this way:

After four weeks of prototype production and laboratory tests, we must now decide whether to forward the wheel assemblies to High

Figure A.2.3
Memo to the Division Vice-president

```
                                          ┌─ Flight tests will
                                          │  be at slower
                                          │  speeds.
                                          │
                                          ├─ Real-life stops
                          ┌─ Life will not be    are at slower
                          │  endangered. ────┤  speeds.
                          │                  │
                          │                  ├─ We can monitor
                          │                  │  tests.              ┌─ We have
   We should send         │                  │                     │  isolated the
   the assemblies  ───────┤                  └─ Defect can be ──────┤  problem.
   to High Flying.        │                     corrected.          │
                          │                                         └─ We can alter
                          │                                            the assembly.
                          │
                          │  ┌─ We can expect
                          └─ We will    │  to get other
                             preserve our  contracts.
                             image and our ──┤
                             economic        │
                             future.         └─ Jobs will be
                                                protected.
```

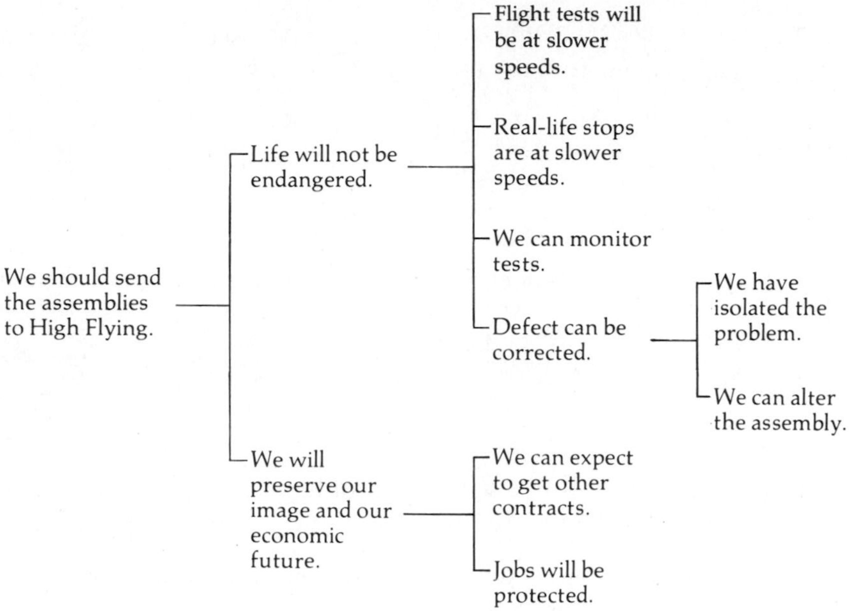

Flying for flight testing. Ordinarily, the decision would be clear-cut. However, in going over the test results, I found certain problems, including unusual wear in certain parts.

Although no one likes to be the bearer of bad news, Russo's coy allusion to "certain problems" will not earn him points with the division vice-president. Although Russo may want to protect his people, this contract is crucial, and the vice-president will not want to wait until page 2 to find out what went wrong. The following opening paragraph tells the vice-president what went wrong and recommends action.

The wheel assembly tests for the High Flying contract are now complete. However, the results reveal that landings at high speeds may cause unexpected wear in parts of the assembly. In spite of this finding we should not delay sending the assemblies. (WHAT) They are serviceable at normal landing speeds, and delay will severely damage Complex's financial status and reputation. (HOW)

Note that there is no WHY IMPORTANT in this opening statement. The vice-president surely knows that this contract is the

Figure A.2.4
Memo to Pilawski

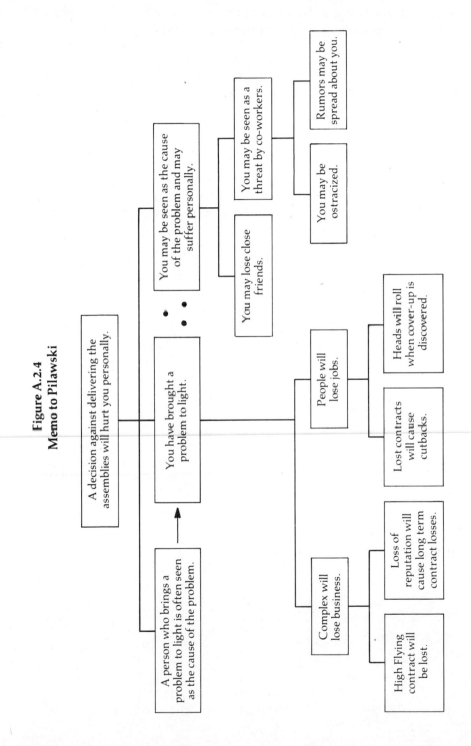

most important thing to happen to the company this year. Telling him about its importance yet again might be viewed as patronizing.

b. Russo might write the introduction to a memo to Pilawski this way:

> Sam, I am writing to you for two reasons.
>
> I have decided not to approve the assembly, and to recommend that we renegotiate our contract based on further strengthening of the assembly. You should be aware of the ramifications of my decision, and how these may affect you. The major effects are the potential financial impact this decision will have on the company and on the personal lives of your co-workers.

Although Russo indicates in this introduction that some problems are in store for Pilawski, he does not say why he thinks so. Pilawski will probably be puzzled by this subtle approach. In a memo based on a deductive argument, the writer should start with the more general idea. In addition, using "Sam" in the beginning may indicate a closer relationship than Russo intends to maintain with his subordinate, even though Russo is trying to get across the idea that "we're all in this together." The following opening is more effective:

> Thank you for sharing with me your misgivings about the safety of the High Flying wheel assembly. I have decided not to approve the test results. (WHAT) Although I know this decision will please you, I am concerned that you may suffer personally as a result of it. (WHY IMPORTANT, HOW)

Chapter 7
First Draft
a.

```
To: VP Production
From: John Russo
Re: High Flying Contract


  The wheel assembly tests for the High Flying con-
tract are now complete. However, the results re-
```

veal that landings at high speeds may cause unexpected wear in parts of the assembly. In spite of
this finding we should not delay sending the assemblies. They are serviceable at normal landing
speeds, and delay will severely damage Complex's
financial status and reputation.

Although there has been some criticism of the way
the tests were handled, the wheel assembly, as it
stands, will meet the requirements of actual
flight testing at High Flying. Simulated tests always exceed the actual requirements of real-life
use. In actuality, any plan landing at the speed
simulated in the high-speed laboratory test would
overshoot the runway and crash regardless of the
strength of the wheel assemblies. As a result, the
flight tests will occur at slower speeds that the
simulated tests and there was no signs of wear in
the assemblies in simulated tests at these speeds.
Furthermore, we can take precautions to monitor
the conditions of the assemblies that we send on
to High Flying. Our technical representatives will
dismantle the wheel assemblies after every actual
flight test to assure that we have not made mistakes in our calculations.

To take care of the design defect my engineers
are working on a way to upgrade the assembly's
strength while remaining within the High Flying's
design specifications. We have isolated the problem and hope to rectify it shortly. The improved
assembly can be phased in immediately.

Although we could opt to delay sending the assemblies, the consequences would be severe. We must
preserve our image as a reliable supplier of high-
technology parts. All our future business depends
on this. If we postpone sending the assemblies, we
will once more have failed to meet our contractual
obligations. The immediate result will be loss of

High Flying's business. Severe though the economic
consequences of this loss may be in terms of layoffs and plant closings, they will be nothing compared with our loss of face in the defense industry. If we fail this time, all doors will be
closed to us.

b.

To: Sam Pilawski
From: John Russo
Re: High Flying Wheel Assembly

Thank you for sharing with me your misgivings
about the safety of the High Flying wheel assembly. I have decided not to approve the test results. Although I know this decision will please
you, I am concerned that you may suffer personally
as a result of it.

You are aware, I am sure, that a person who
brings a problem to light is often seen as the
cause of that problem. We may lose the High Flying
contract. This can mean extremely tough financial
times in the short run as much of our growth has
been planned around the successful completion of
this contract and the opening of new markets which
we hoped would ensue. Many, especially those in
senior management, view this contract as essential
to the life of Complex. In addition, our reputation and therefore long term business may be lost.

The lives of your co-workers may be seriously
affected by the loss of the contract. This means a
loss of promotions, a possible closing of career

options, and most significantly a loss of work for
many in the Complex family.

   I realize that you did not create the problem and
I admire your courage and perserverance in pursu-
ing it. I do feel however that I should warn you
that you may lose friends as people will see you
as threatening their job security. I trust you
will successfully handle what may be a rather unpleasant situation.

Chapter 8

Some memos do not lend themselves to the use of headings. The
draft of the memo from Russo to Pilawski in chapter 7 is quite
short and therefore does not need headings. The memo from Russo to the division vice-president is also short. Furthermore, it presents an argument that the writer might not care to have "jump off
the page." For examples of good uses of headings, see the revised
memos for the Budget Finance case in this appendix.

Chapter 9

Revising the Memo.
a.

To: VP Production
From: John Russo
Re: High Flying Contract

   The wheel assembly tests for the High Flying con-

tract are now complete. However, the results reveal

that landings at high speeds may cause unexpected

wear in parts of the assembly. In spite of this

finding we should not delay sending the assemblies.

They are serviceable at normal landing speeds,

and delay will severely damage Complex's financial

status and reputation.

~~Although there has been some criticism of the way~~

~~the tests were handled,~~ the wheel assembly, as it

stands, will ~~meet the requirements of actual~~ pass the

flight testing at High Flying. Simulated tests ~~al-~~
create greater stress than flight tests or actual
~~ways exceed the actual requirements of real life~~

use; ~~In actuality,~~ any plane landing at the speed

simulated in the high-speed laboratory test would

overshoot the runway and crash regardless of the

strength of the wheel assemblies. ~~As a result, the~~

~~flight tests will occur at slower speeds that the~~

The ~~Our~~ tests did not reveal any irregular wear ~~in the wheel assemblies~~
~~simulated tests and there was no signs of wear in~~

~~the assemblies in simulated tests~~ at these slower speeds.

Furthermore, ~~we can take precautions to monitor~~

~~the conditions of the assemblies that we send on~~

~~to High Flying;~~ our technical representatives will

dismantle the wheel assemblies after every ~~actual~~

test at High Flying in that our calculations are not mistaken.

My engineers are working on a way to correct the design defect without violating the specifications of the contract. We have isolated the problem and hope to correct it shortly. The improved assembly can be phased in as soon as it is ready.

Although we could delay sending the assemblies, failing to meet the contract deadline would be disastrous. We must preserve our image as a reliable supplier of high-technology parts. All our future business depends on it. If we fail to meet our contractual obligations this time, the immediate result will be the loss of High Flying's business. Severe though the economic consequences of this may be in terms of layoffs and plant closings, they will be nothing compared with the long term loss of business if we forfeit our reputation for reliability. If we fail this time, all doors will be closed to us.

To: VP Production
From: John Russo
Re: High Flying Contract

   The wheel assembly tests for the High Flying contract are now complete. However, the results reveal that landings at high speeds may cause unexpected wear in parts of the assembly. In spite of
this finding we should not delay sending the assemblies. They are serviceable at normal landing
speeds, and delay will severely damage Complex's
financial status and reputation.
   The wheel assembly, as it stands, will pass the
flight test at High Flying. Simulated tests create
greater stress than flight tests or actual use;
any plane landing at the speed simulated in the
high-speed laboratory test would overshoot the
runway and crash regardless of the strength of the
wheel assemblies. The tests did not reveal any
irregular wear at these slower speeds. Furthermore, our technical representatives will dismantle
the wheel assemblies after every test at High
Flying to insure that our calculations are not
mistaken.
   My engineers are working on a way to correct the
design defect without violating the specifications
of the contract. We have isolated the problem and
hope to correct it shortly. The improved assembly
can be phased in as soon as it is ready.
   Although we could delay sending the assemblies,
failing to meet the contract deadline would be
disastrous. We must preserve our image as a reliable supplier of high-technology parts. All our
future business depends on it. If we fail to meet
our contractual obligations this time, the immediate result will be loss of High Flying's busi-

ness. Severe though the economic consequences of
this may be in terms of layoffs and plant closings,
they will be nothing compared with the long-term
loss of business if we forfeit our reputation for
reliability. If we fail this time, all doors will
be closed to us.

To: Sam Pilawski
From: John Russo
Re: High Flying Wheel Assembly

Thank you for sharing with me your misgivings

about the safety of the High Flying wheel assem-

bly. I have decided not to approve the test re-

sults. Although I know this decision will please

you, I am concerned that you may suffer personally

as a result of it.
As you probably realize,
~~You are aware, I am sure,~~ ~~that~~ a person who

brings a problem to light is often seen as the
(Because of your report, and my decision, Complex)
cause of that problem. ~~We~~ may lose the High Flying
          loss   severely damage the company
contract. This can ~~mean extremely tough financial~~
                    we have expanded to produce
~~times~~ in the short run; ~~as much of our growth has~~
these assemblies and to enter the new markets
~~been planned around the successful completion of~~
the High Flying contract would open for us.
~~this contract and the opening of new markets which~~

~~we hoped would ensue~~ Many, *of our senior managers* ~~especially those in~~

~~senior management~~ view thi*e*s contract as essential

company's survival. to the ~~life of Complex~~ In addition, ~~our~~ *loss of this contract* reputa-

(run on) *will tarnish our* tion ~~and therefore~~ *for meeting* ~~our~~ commitments ~~and~~ long term business may ~~be lost~~ *suffer as well.*

As a result, The lives of your co-workers *could* ~~may~~ be seriously

affected. ~~by the loss of the contract. This means a~~ *Some could forfeit* *more could lose their jobs.* ~~loss of~~ promotions; ~~a possible closing of career~~

~~options, and most significantly a loss of work for~~

~~many in the Complex family~~

I realize that you did not create the problem and

I admire your courage and persev^erance in ~~pursu~~ *reporting*

~~ing~~ it. I ~~do feel however that I should warn you~~ *should warn you, however,*

that *and coworkers are likely to* ~~that you may lose~~ friends ~~as people will~~ see you

as *a* threaten*to*~~ing~~ their job security. ~~I trust~~ you *Although I am sure* *that*

will successfully handle ~~what may be a rather~~ *any* un-

pleasant ~~situation~~ *ness that arises, I'd like you to know* *you can count on my support.*

To: Sam Pilawski
From: John Russo
Re: High Flying Wheel Assembly

  Thank you for sharing with me your misgivings
about the safety of the High Flying wheel assembly. I have decided not to approve the test results. Although I know this decision will please
you, I am concerned that you may suffer personally
as a result of it.
  As you probably realize, a person who brings a
problem to light is often seen as the cause of
that problem. Because of your report, and my decision, Complex may lose the High Flying contract.
This loss can severely damage the company in the
short run; we have expanded to produce these assemblies and to enter the new markets the High
Flying contract would open for us. Many of our
senior managers view the contract as essential to
the company's survival. In addition, loss of this
contract will tarnish our reputation for meeting
commitments—long-term business may suffer as
well. As a result, the lives of your co-workers
could be seriously affected. Some could forfeit
promotions; many could lose their jobs.
  I realize that you did not create the problem,
and I admire your courage and perseverance in reporting it. I should warn you, however, that
friends and co-workers are likely to see you as a
threat to their job security. Although I am sure
that you will successfully handle any unpleasantness that arises, I'd like you to know you can
count on my support.

Budget Finance Corporation

Chapter 2

Lerue might have focused on his reader as shown below.

Reader Guideline

Subject of the report or memo: *Budget Finance Loan*
Name of the primary reader: *Investment Committee*
Question the reader might ask: *Should the bank make this loan?*
My position in relation to the primary reader:
—professional: *The committee makes the decision.*
—personal: *Some are friends, some aren't.*
How extensive is his or her knowledge of the subject: (great, minimal, nonexistent—describe)   *Committee members know a great deal about loans, but they don't know Budget's figures.*
What are his or her biases about the subject?   *Most are committed to increasing bank's visibility in low-income areas.*
What are his or her significant managerial traits and stylistic preferences?   *Most members like brief reports with supporting evidence.*
Who are the secondary readers?   *None*
Is anyone else likely to receive this report?   *Board of Directors*

Chapter 3

To answer the question of whether the bank should buy the debentures, Lerue must first decide if the investment is sound—if the company will be able to repay the debt. He might develop the tree shown in figure A.2.5 as the basis for his research. Or Lerue might develop an analysis tree based on what he believes are the bank's criteria for making a loan (see figure A.2.6).

Lerue might establish these criteria:

Figure A.2.5

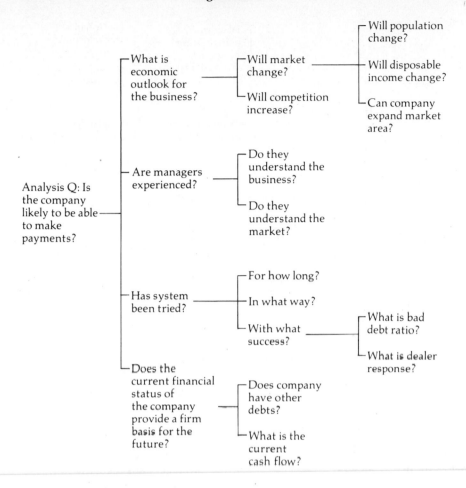

Limit of Freedom

The company will not default in the fore-seeable future.

Reason

Bank policy

Negotiable Criteria: (ranked on a scale of 1–5 with 5 the most significant)

Criteria	Weight	Reason for Weight
The investment must increase bank visibility in the community.	5	Senior management is committed to participating in development of low-income communities in ways that improve the bank's image.
The company will keep an average monthly balance of $100,000 in checking account.	3	We are not, currently, as concerned with balances as with community visibility.

Figure A.2.6

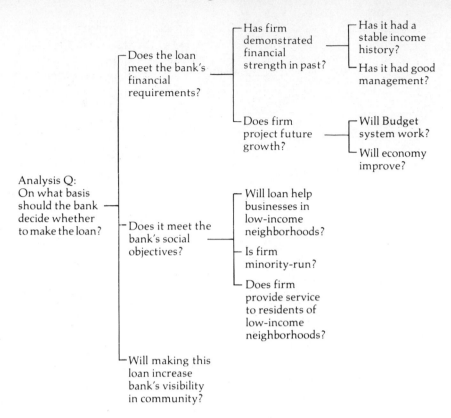

Financial ratios are not currently below industry averages.	2	We have been accepting below-average ratios regularly from low-income area businesses.
The investment must help companies in low-income neighborhoods.	4	Bank is committed to helping the community grow.

a. Lerue might decide that he accepts Ephram's figures and that analysis shows the company will not default on the loan. Since the loan meets the limit of freedom, he would continue:

Alternative: Make loan

	Value	(X Criteria Weight)	Reason
Investment will increase visibility. (5)	5	25	We can develop billboard and TV advertising with principals.

Company will keep adequate average balances. (3)	3	9	At first, company will need all the available cash to expand.
Financial ratios meet industry average. (2)	0	0	Ratios don't equal industry average.
Investment will help companies in community. (4)	4	16	Support for this company will filter funds to other neighborhood businesses.
Total score		50	

In this instance, if there are no better alternative uses for the funds, Lerue would recommend making the loan since not making it would have a total score of zero.

b. If Lerue decides the proposal does not meet the limit of freedom, he does not need to continue the analysis. Even if the loan meets the limit of freedom, if it has a low score (as it does in the following evaluation), he may choose not to recommend it.

Alternative: Deny loan

	Value	(X Criteria Weight)	Reason
Investment will increase visibility. (5)	2	10	Potential for advertising is small.
Company will keep adequate average balances. (3)	0	0	Record shows Budget does not have enough cash to maintain balances.
Financial ratios meet industry average. (2)	0	0	Ratios don't equal industry average.
Investment will help companies in community. (4)	0	0	This loan will not help other businesses.
Total score		10	

Chapter 4

a. If he decides to recommend the loan, Lerue might group his assertions this way:

Assertions	Generalizations
Management has ten years experience in the business. Management understands the market and communicates in Spanish.	Management is in a good position to succeed in this business.
Population is expected to grow rapidly in market area. Welfare income is expected to increase. Economy is expected to improve.	With more money available, demand for loans should increase.
Bank can suggest that convertible feature of debentures indicates its interest in future ownership. Size of operation will give bank broad exposure. TV commercials with the Spanish-speaking partner will provide good publicity.	Bank can use this loan to indicate its commitment to the community.
Business is expected to approximately double between 1973 and 1977. Although high, expenses are commensurate with growth. Income will more than cover interest on debentures. Computer system has been effective to date in forestalling increase in bad debts.	Financial projections appear sound.

Several of these groupings about the company's ability to repay might be further grouped when the ideas are ordered to look like this:

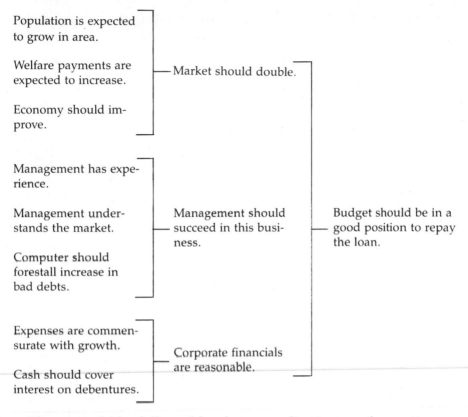

These would be followed by the generalizations and assertions about community commitment:

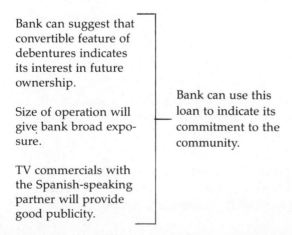

In this case, the recommendation should come first. That is what the investment committee wants to know. Lerue does not need to support his criteria because he is convinced that the investment committee members will accept them. The most important criterion is that the loan is fiscally sound, so discussion of economics should come first.

b. If Lerue decides to recommend denial of the loan, he might group his assertions this way:

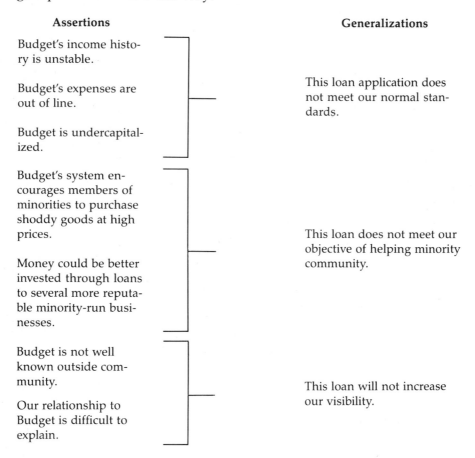

Assertions	Generalizations
Budget's income history is unstable.	
Budget's expenses are out of line.	This loan application does not meet our normal standards.
Budget is undercapitalized.	
Budget's system encourages members of minorities to purchase shoddy goods at high prices.	This loan does not meet our objective of helping minority community.
Money could be better invested through loans to several more reputable minority-run businesses.	
Budget is not well known outside community.	This loan will not increase our visibility.
Our relationship to Budget is difficult to explain.	

These assertions would, of course, be supported by data. This grouping could provide the structure for the memo.

Chapter 5

Lerue might picture his argument as in figure A.2.7, based on his assertions in support of making the loan. Note that he refines the grouping and ordering further in organizing his argument.

Figure A.2.7

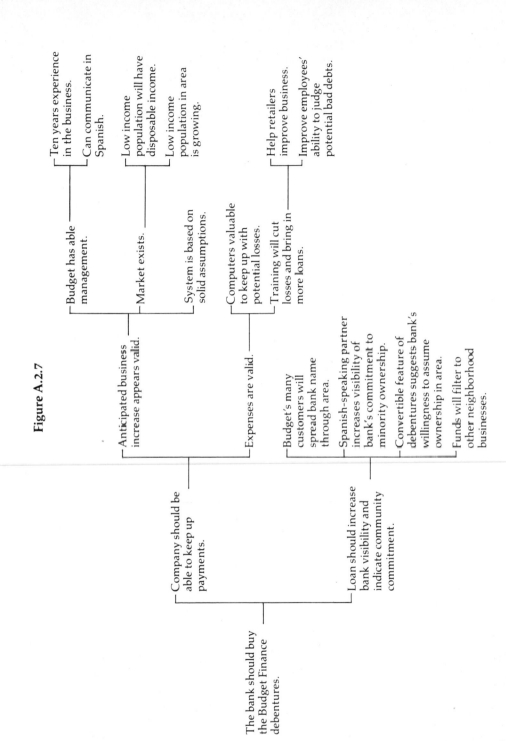

The bank should buy the Budget Finance debentures.

Company should be able to keep up payments.

Anticipated business increase appears valid.

Budget has able management.
- Ten years experience in the business.
- Can communicate in Spanish.

Market exists.
- Low income population will have disposable income.
- Low income population in area is growing.

System is based on solid assumptions.

Expenses are valid.

Computers valuable to keep up with potential losses.

Training will cut losses and bring in more loans.
- Help retailers improve business.
- Improve employees' ability to judge potential bad debts.

Loan should increase bank visibility and indicate community commitment.

Budget's many customers will spread bank name through area.

Spanish-speaking partner increases visibility of bank's commitment to minority ownership.

Convertible feature of debentures suggests bank's willingness to assume ownership in area.

Funds will filter to other neighborhood businesses.

Figure A.2.8

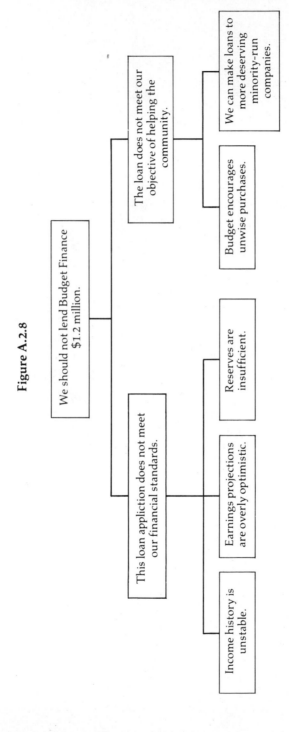

In arguing against the loan, Lerue might develop the pyramid shown in figure A.2.8.

Chapter 6

a. Lerue might write this introduction for the memo recommending that the bank make the loan:

> Some months ago, Robert Ephram approached me with the proposal that the bank purchase $1.2 million of convertible debentures in Budget Finance Corporation, a small-loan company with offices in several low-income neighborhoods in the greater metropolitan area. He argued that the loan fits our advertised goal of participating in the revitalization of these neighborhoods. I have worked with him on the development of the financial data before you, and I believe that such a loan can be supported on the grounds that it meets both our financial and social criteria.

Looking at it critically, Lerue could decide that the Investment Committee is not interested in how long he had been meeting with Robert Ephram or in the nature of Ephram's arguments. He would then rewrite the introduction this way (fixing some of the wording at the same time):

> At its next meeting, the Committee must decide (WHY IMPORTANT) whether to approve the purchase of $1.2 million of convertible debentures in Budget Finance Corporation, a financial services company that buys commercial paper from retailers in low-income neighborhoods. (WHAT) I recommend that we approve this loan: it both meets our financial criteria and advances us toward our advertised goal of participating in the revitalization of low-income areas. (HOW)

b. For his modified outline memo recommending against the loan, Lerue might start out with a simple one-sentence introduction:

> I recommend against making a $1.2 million loan to Budget Finance Corporation.

Because he is distributing this memo to the committee members just before the meeting and will make a presentation, he may think he can fill in the gaps orally. Furthermore, the committee will know why the subject is significant—they are, after all, meeting to make a decision on it. He might decide, though, that his short beginning is a bit harsh, and rewrite it this way:

> Based on my analysis of the Budget Finance Corporation financial statements, my meetings with Robert Ephram, Budget's president, and my view of the economic future of New York, I recommend that we do not purchase the $1.2 million in convertible debentures. (WHAT) The company's financial record does not meet our minimum standards for investment. Furthermore, the loan would not meet our objective of aiding the minority community. (HOW)

Chapter 7

First Draft
a.

```
To:  Investment Committee
From: John Lerue
Re: Budget Finance Loan

   At its next meeting, the Committee must decide
whether to approve the purchase of $1.2 million of
convertible debentures in Budget Finance Corpora-
tion, a financial services company that buys com-
mercial paper from retailers in low-income neigh-
borhoods. I recommend that we approve this loan:
it both meets our financial criteria and advances
us toward our advertised goal of participating in
the revitalization of low-income areas.
   Budget Finance should be sufficiently strong to
meet the payments on the debentures. Anticipated
business increases appear valid based on the
strength of management and on the growing market.
With ten years experience, Ephram has developed
a program that should attract retailers to do
```

business with him. He seems to have judged the
problems of the industry well and to have established ways to overcome the past problems of shoddy merchandise, poor follow-up on bad debts and
poor selection of potential customers. In addition, the bilingual experience of employees, and
particularly the bilingual abilities of one of the
principals, should bring in new business.

At the same time, the market is expected to improve. As the population in the neighborhoods
where Budget is based grows and as welfare payments increase and the general level of employment
improves, there should be substantially more disposable income in the area.

Although the figures indicate that Budget's expenses are quite high relative to income for the
next few years, these expenditures should provide
the base for further income growth. The installation of new computers should help limit the losses
that are considered a part of this business by
permitting management to keep abreast of any
changes in the economy that affect its market. The
training expenditures planned by Budget will serve
both its employees and the retailers with whom the
company does business. The retailers should improve their business, and therefore Budget's income, through this training and the company employees should be in a better position to judge
poor prospects as a result of this experience. The
combination of management experience, solid systems, well-spent training and computer funds, and
a growing economy should provide Budget with more
than enough funds to repay its debt to the bank.

At the same time, making this loan will increase

the bank's visibility in the low-income areas
where the company is situated and indicate our
commitment to helping the community grow. The size
of the Budget operation permits us exposure in
almost every area in which we are interested. And
as the company grows that exposure will increase.
We anticipate some joint advertising that should
serve us both well. We have been looking, for some
time, for a chance to participate in an organization that has a Spanish-speaking partner. In addition, the convertible feature of the debenture
will suggest to the community that we have an interest in owning property in the area.

The training programs Budget will run will have a
ripple effect in the community as other organizations gain from their exposure to Budget's ideas
and as Budget provides funds to retailers that
will increase their sales.

The loan will serve the bank and will serve the
community.

b.

To: Investment Committee
From: John Lerue
Re: Budget Finance Loan

Based on my analysis of the Budget Finance Corporation financial statements, my meetings with Robert Ephram, Budget's president, and my view of the

economic future of New York, I recommend that we
do not purchase the $1.2 million in convertible
debentures. The company's financial record does
not meet our minimum standards for investment.
Furthermore, the loan would not meet our objective
of aiding the minority community.

This loan does not meet normal standards for investment.

- Budget Finance's income history has been unstable.
- The company's income and expense projections
  are unrealistic.
  —Expense projections are massive.
  —Income projections are unrealistic.
- Budget's reserves are insufficient to weather
  any economic downturn.
  —Even with this loan, Budget will be undercapi-
  talized.
  —Although the national economic outlook is excellent, New York City, particularly the area
  in which Budget operates, may not share in
  this growth and may even suffer a further economic erosion.
  —Although Budget has an impressive management
  team, their expertise cannot compensate for
  the first three deficiencies.

This loan does not meet our objective of aiding
the minority community.

- The Budget system encourages minority residents
  to purchase shoddy merchandise on credit at
  inflated prices.
- The $1.2 million could be divided among several
  better-run businesses in the community.
  —We have requests pending.
  —We can seek new prospects.

Chapter 8

Most frequently, writers add headings as they revise. The answers to the chapter 9 exercises include a revised memo with headings.

a. If Lerue were making a recommendation for the loan, he might want visuals with these headings:
1. Budget expenses, although high, will contribute to earnings.
   [*Line graph of expenses and income projections.*]
2. Budget locations are near bank branches.
   [*Map showing area Budget serves and bank branch locations.*]

b. If Lerue were making a presentation supporting a memo recommending against making the loan, he might want visuals titled as follows:
1. Budget Finance's income history has been unstable.
   [*Bar chart showing income since firm's founding.*]
2. Budget projections are unrealistic.
   [*Overlay to first chart showing projected income.*]

Chapter 9

Revising the Memo
a.

To: Investment Committee
From: John Lerue
Re: Budget Finance Loan

At its next meeting, the Committee must decide whether to approve the purchase of $1.2 million of convertible debentures in Budget Finance Corporation, a financial services company that buys commercial paper from retailers in low-income neighborhoods. I recommend that we approve this loan:

it both meets our financial criteria and advances

us toward our advertised goal of participating in

the revitalization of low-income areas.

Budget's Application Meets Our Financial Criteria

Budget Finance should be able to make payments on schedule. The anticipated increase in business seems reasonable, given Budget's strong management and projected market growth. Drawing on his ten years' experience, Ephram has developed a program that should attract retailers and overcome the industry's traditional problems—shoddy merchandise, inadequate follow-up on defaults, and poor selection of potential customers. In addition, his bilingual partner and employees should attract new business in the Spanish-speaking community. The retail market is expected to improve as the population in the neighborhoods Budget's retailers serve in the area grows and as welfare payments and employment increase.

~~improves, there should be substantially more~~ dis-

posable income in the area *& should keep pace, justifying* *Budget's* ~~forecasts~~.

Although ~~the figures indicate that~~ Budget's ex-

penses ~~are quite~~ *will be* high relative to income for the

next ~~few~~ *four* years *(see exhibit 1),* these expenditures ~~should provide~~ *will lay* *foundation*

the ~~base~~ for further income growth. The installa-

tion of ~~new~~ computers should help limit the losses

usually associated with the finance

~~that are considered a part of this~~ business .~~by~~

~~permitting management to keep abreast of any~~

~~changes in the economy that affect its market.~~ The

proposed

training ~~expenditures planned by Budget will serve~~ *programs will help*

~~both its employees and the retailers with whom the~~

~~company does business. The~~ retailers ~~should~~ im-

practices

prove their business and ~~therefore Budget's in-~~

give

~~come, through this training and the~~ company em-

the expertise to make informed decisions and

ployees ~~should be in a better position to judge~~

weed out

poor prospects. ~~as a result of this experience. The~~

The company's combinat~~ion of~~ management, experience, ~~solid~~ *innovative* sys-

and

tems, ~~well spent~~ training and computer ~~funds and~~ a *programs, combined* *with*

easily

growing economy, should provide Budget with ~~more~~

the cashflow necessary

~~than enough funds~~ to repay its debt to the bank.

The Loan Will Aid the Minority Community

~~At the same time,~~ making ^a this loan will ~~increase~~
be a visible symbol of / commitment to helping
^the bank's ~~visibility~~ ~~in the~~ low-income areas.

~~where the company is situated and indicate our~~

~~commitment to helping the community grow. The size~~
is involved
~~of the~~ Budget ~~operation permits us exposure~~ in
neighborhood   have a branch.   (See ex-
almost every ~~area~~ in which we ~~are interested. And~~   hibit
And, as   expands, our   also   2)
~~as~~ the company ~~grows that~~ exposure will also increase.

~~We anticipate some~~ joint advertising, ~~that should~~
both print
and TV, will reinforce this tie.
~~serve us both well. We have been looking, for some~~

~~time, for a chance to participate in an organiza-~~

~~tion that has a Spanish-speaking partner.~~ In addi-
because the debentures are
tion, ~~the~~ convertible, ~~feature of the debenture~~
acquiring them will demonstrate the bank's
~~will suggest to the community that we have an~~ in-
participating
terest in ~~owning property~~ in the ~~area~~   ownership of local
Budget's   and the loan itself   business.
~~The~~ training programs ~~Budget will run~~ will have a

ripple effect; ~~in the~~ community ~~as other organiza-~~
retailers will improve their management skills and
~~tions gain from their exposure to Budget's ideas~~
(will channel the bank's)   indirectly
~~and as~~ Budget ~~provides~~ funds to retailers, ~~that~~
contributing to increased   their
~~will increase their~~ sales.
to Budget, then,
The loan will serve the bank and ~~will serve~~ the

community.

To: Investment Committee
From: John Lerue
Re: Budget Finance Loan

At its next meeting, the Committee must decide
whether to approve the purchase of $1.2 million of
convertible debentures in Budget Finance Corporation, a financial services company that buys commercial paper from retailers in low-income neighborhoods. I recommend that we approve this loan:
it both meets our financial criteria and advances
us toward our advertised goal of participating in
the revitalization of low-income areas.

Budget's Application Meets Our Financial Criteria

Budget Finance should be able to make payments on
schedule. The anticipated increase in business
seems reasonable, given Budget's strong management
and projected market growth. Drawing on his ten
years' experience, Ephram has developed a program
that should attract retailers and overcome the
industry's traditional problems--shoddy merchandise, inadequate follow-up on defaults, and poor
selection of potential customers. In addition, his
bilingual partner and employees should attract new
business in the Spanish-speaking community.

The retail market in the neighborhoods Budget's
retailers serve is expected to improve as population in the area grows and as welfare payments and
employment increase. Disposable income in the area
should keep pace, justifying Budget's forecasts.

Although Budget's expenses will be high relative
to income for the next four years (see exhibit 1),
these expenditures will lay the foundation for
further income growth. The installation of computers should help limit the losses usually asso-

ciated with the finance business. The proposed
training programs will help retailers improve
their business practices and give company employees the expertise to make informed decisions and
weed out poor prospects. The company's experienced
management, innovative system, and training and
computer programs, combined with a growing economy, should easily provide Budget with the cash
flow necessary to repay its debt to the bank.

The Loan Will Aid the Minority Community

This loan will be a visible symbol of the bank's
commitment to helping low-income areas. Budget is
involved in almost every neighborhood in which we
have a branch (see exhibit 2). And, as the company
expands, our exposure will also increase. Joint
advertising, both print and TV, will reinforce
this tie. In addition, because the debentures are
convertible, acquiring them will demonstrate the
bank's interest in participating in the ownership
of local business.

Budget's training programs and the loan itself
will have a ripple effect; community retailers
will improve their management skills and Budget
will channel the bank's funds to retailers, indirectly contributing to their increased sales.

The loan to Budget, then, will serve the bank and
the community.

b.

To: Investment Committee
From: John Lerue
Re: Budget Finance Loan

   Based on my analysis of the Budget Finance Corpo-

ration financial statements, my meetings with Rob-

ert Ephram, Budget's president, and my view of the

economic future of New York, I recommend that we

do not purchase the $1.2 million in convertible

debentures. The company's financial record does

not meet our minimum standards for investment.

Furthermore, the loan would not meet our objective

of aiding the minority community.
                      application   *our minimum*
   This loan ^ does not meet ~~normal~~ ^ standards ~~o for in~~

~~vestment~~

                              has had an unstable
• Budget Finance ^'s income history. ~~has been unsta~~

~~ble.~~

                          earnings
• The company's ~~income and expense~~ projections
        too optimistic. ^
are ~~unrealistic~~
     Computerization and training *cannot bring in the*
~~Expense projections are massive~~ *new business Budget*
                                              predicts.

~~Income projections are unrealistic~~

- Budget ~~'s reserves are insufficient~~ *is not strong enough* to weather an~~y~~ economic downturn.
  - *— Budget's ratio of expenses to income is excessively high.*
  - —Even with ~~this loan~~ *the funds provided by*, Budget will be undercapi- talized.

  —Although the national economic outlook is ex-

  cellent, New York City, particularly the area

  in which Budget operates, may not share in

  this growth and may even suffer further eco-

  nomic erosion.

- ~~Although~~ Budget has an impressive management

  team, ~~their~~ *its* expertise cannot compensate for

  the first three deficiencies.

This loan does not meet our objective of aiding

the minority community.

- The Budget system encourages minority residents

  to purchase shoddy merchandise on credit at

  inflated prices.

- The $1.2 million could be divided among several

  ~~better run~~ *community* businesses ~~in the community~~ *that are better risks than Budget.*

  —We have *twelve* requests pending.

  —We can seek new prospects.

To: Investment Committee
From: John Lerue
Re: Budget Finance Loan

Based on my analysis of the Budget Finance Corporation financial statements, my meetings with Robert Ephram, Budget's president, and my view of the
economic future of New York, I recommend that we
do not purchase the $1.2 million in convertible
debentures. The company's financial record does
not meet our minimum standards for investment.
Furthermore, the loan would not meet our objective
of aiding the minority community.

This loan application does not meet our minimum
standards.

- Budget Finance has had an unstable income his-
  tory.
- The company's earnings projections are too op-
  timistic.
  - Computerization and training cannot bring in
    the new business Budget predicts.
  - Although the national economic outlook is ex-
    cellent, New York City, particularly the area
    in which Budget operates, may not share in
    this growth and may even suffer further eco-
    nomic erosion.
- Budget is not strong enough to weather an eco-
  nomic downturn.
  - Budget's ratio of expenses to income is exces-
    sively high.
  - Even with the funds provided by this loan,
    Budget will be undercapitalized.
- Although Budget has an impressive management
  team, management's expertise cannot compensate
  for the first three deficiencies.

This loan does not meet our objective of aiding the minority community.
- The Budget system encourages minority residents to purchase shoddy merchandise on credit at inflated prices.
- The $1.2 million could be divided among several community businesses that are better risks than Budget.

  —We have twelve requests pending.

  —We can seek new prospects.

3

PROBLEM SOLVING AND GROUPING EXAMPLES

Analysis Tree Exercises

Here are several cases in which managers used analysis trees to be certain they had all the components of a whole or to isolate a problem or opportunity. Each example indicates one way to approach the situation. You might choose another way, but by testing your thinking against another manager's you will become more practiced at using the analysis-tree technique.

Example 1

The president of a construction company involved with the renovation of historically interesting buildings asked his assistant to tell him about the new housing commissioner. The assistant stated the question he thought was really in the president's mind as, "What are the new housing commissioner's views on renovation?" He could not interview the commissioner and had to use secondary sources for information. He decided that if he knew the commissioner's experiences, biases, and knowledge about renovation he might be able to answer the president's question. He therefore put the analysis question "What might indicate the housing commissioner's experience, biases and knowledge about renovation?" on the left side of the sheet and formed the analysis tree in figure A.3.1 by asking further questions that might answer the analysis question. How would you develop the tree?

Example 2

The division head of a manufacturing company was asked to evaluate three locations for a small-parts assembly plant. He decided that the decision would be based on the proximity to the com-

Figure A.3.1
Analysis Tree

Question: What are the new housing commissioner's views on renovation?

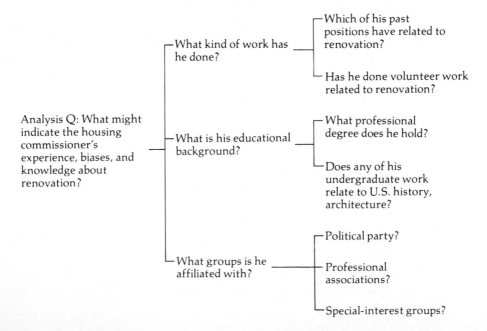

**Figure A.3.2
Analysis Tree**

Question: What are the advantages and disadvantages of three possible locations for a small-parts assembly?

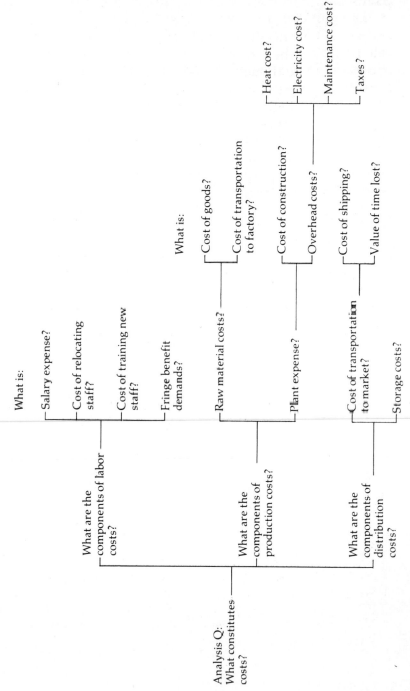

Analysis Q:
What constitutes
costs?

- What are the components of labor costs?
  - What is:
    - Salary expense?
    - Cost of relocating staff?
    - Cost of training new staff?
    - Fringe benefit demands?
- What are the components of production costs?
  - What is:
    - Raw material costs?
      - Cost of goods?
      - Cost of transportation to factory?
    - Plant expense?
      - Cost of construction?
      - Overhead costs?
        - Heat cost?
        - Electricity cost?
        - Maintenance cost?
        - Taxes?
- What are the components of distribution costs?
  - Cost of transportation to market?
    - Cost of shipping?
    - Value of time lost?
  - Storage costs?

pany's largest market, the availability of labor, and the costs of operating in each location. A map would indicate proximity to market and census data would indicate whether there was an available labor force, but to determine costs he developed the analysis tree in figure A.3.2 beginning on the left with this question: "What constitutes costs?" Test your analytical skills against his.

Grouping Exercise

The consultant, asked to determine why candy profits were down, established that fixed costs had held steady and that the candy's unit contribution was in line with that of the company's other products. But sales volume was off substantially. In looking for the cause of the sales decline, she made a number of tentative conclusions based on inferences about the data. She believed the sales decline was caused by a population drop and competition from candy alternatives. As a result, she was inclined to suggest that the company should develop a health food bar. Looking at the answers to the questions on the analysis tree she used to solve her original problem, she made this list of statements that related in some way to the decline in candy sales and might support her argument:

All our competitors in the candy industry have increased advertising in youth magazines.

Advertising of all types for candy alternatives is up 25 percent.

We offered four new candy bars in the market this year.

Competitors' sales of their older brands of candy are down.

Advertising for candy alternatives is saturating TV during family viewing time.

One of our competitors has developed extensive shopping-center promotions.

The twelve-to-eighteen-year-old population has held even for the past three years.

The twelve-and-under population has declined 25 percent in the past three years.

Sales of all new types of candy are slow.

The population of the eighteen-and-older age group has declined 10 percent over a five-year period.

Parent groups favor candy alternatives.

Sales of candy alternatives are up.

The birth rate is expected to drop in the next ten years.

Some of these statements are assertions and some are supporting evidence. It is much harder to group someone else's ideas than to group your own, but it is good practice. This is how the consultant grouped her assertions:

Assertion 1:   Total population in the area is down.

Support: The population of people eighteen years and older has declined 10 percent over a five-year period.

The population of twelve-to-eighteen-year-olds has stayed the same for the past three years.

The twelve-and-under group has declined 25 percent in the past three years.

She considered placing the evidence about the declining birth rate in this group, but she realized that this statement, unlike the others, related to the future, so she did not use it here. The category is complete as it stands. All age groups are discussed; the "total" portion of the assertion has been supported.

She then looked for evidence to support the idea that increased competition caused the decline. There were two kinds of competition: candy and candy alternatives such as granola munchies and yogurt sticks.

Assertion 2:   Sales of candy alternatives are up.

She had statistical proof for this, which she set aside for an exhibit. The assertions that advertising for these items is up 25 percent, that it is saturating TV during family viewing time, and that parent groups prefer alternatives all relate to the increase in sales, but they do not prove that sales are up and so do not support the assertion.

The consultant wanted to be certain the reader did not assume that sales were being lost to other candy products, an idea she believed management held.

> Assertion 3:   Our competitors' sales of candy are down despite extensive efforts.
>
> Support: All our competitors have increased their advertising in youth magazines.
>
> One competitor has done shopping center promotions.

The consultant then had these assertions to support her conclusion that population decline and candy alternative sales were the cause of the sales decline.

> Assertion 1:   Total population in the area is down.
>
> Assertion 2:   Sales of candy alternatives are up.
>
> Assertion 3:   Our competitors' candy sales are down despite extensive efforts.

With support organized for her conclusions about why profits were down, the consultant turned to grouping arguments to support her recommendation that:

The company should develop a new health food bar.

Her reasons were:

> Assertion 1:   Our candy sales will continue to drop.
>
> Support: People will continue to buy candy alternatives.
>
> Parent groups favor candy alternatives.
>
> Candy alternative advertising is reaching a large part of the population. (Expenditures are up, alternatives are being advertised heavily on family TV shows.)

The dropping birth rate means there will be fewer people in the age groups that buy the most candy. Each of these points is an extrapolation from her facts.

<u>Assertion 2:</u>   We can easily convert our facilities to make candy alternatives.

<u>Assertion 3:</u>   Candy alternatives are profitable.

Both of the last two assertions are supported with exhibits or charts showing how to convert the factory to make candy alternatives and providing earning projections for the candy alternatives she recommends—information you do not have.

APPENDIX

4

SECONDARY
SOURCES

The secondary sources you use regularly will depend on your position in the hierarchy and on the industry or agency in which you are working. It is a good idea to organize a list if you are just beginning. Be sure to consider the following categories.

Newspapers: This category includes major dailies and trade papers. Many provide regular indexes to their articles.

Professional Journals: Lists of these are available through professional organizations and by checking the *Guide to Business Periodicals*.

Regional Journals and Magazines: Many of these can provide useful information about your area.

Business Operating Guides: The titles of these should be available from your professional association.

Directories of Corporations: The most obvious members of this category are *Dunn and Bradstreet* and *Standard and Poor*. Others are available from federal, state, and local governments, from chambers of commerce, and from professional organizations.

U.S. Government Periodicals: These probably provide more statistical data than any one manager could ever use. Many libraries keep lists of available federal documents. Complete lists and prices are available from the Superintendent of Documents, Government Printing Office, Washington, D.C. Although it takes time, it is well worth the effort to discover what is available in your field of interest.

Annual Reports: Annual reports are public documents; you should be able to get the annual reports of your competitors simply by asking. Annual reports for corporations in your immediate area may be available through the chamber of commerce.

A good hunting ground for all kinds of secondary sources is Bernice and Terry Nelson's *Basic Library Reference Sources* (1975), available through the Government Printing Office.

5

WRITING
CHECKLISTS AND
GUIDELINES

Assembled here for your reference and use are selected checklists and guidelines that appeared in the text and that represent key steps in the managerial writing process. Read through them as a quick review or refer to them individually as you confront a particular task in your writing.

Writing Checklist

	Yes	No	Not Sure
1. Who will take action on the basis of this memo? Is the memo written to convince the primary reader?	_____	_____	_____
2. Is it clear *why* you are writing?	_____	_____	_____
3. Do you tell the reader, within the first few sentences, the one major point and the supporting points you intend to make?	_____	_____	_____
4. Do you limit your discussion to those points?	_____	_____	_____
5. Do you answer the questions that are likely to come to the reader's mind when he or she reads the memo? These are likely to be questions beginning with "how" or "why."	_____	_____	_____
6. Have you grouped your supporting ideas in a way that makes the fewest, most significant points?	_____	_____	_____
7. Do you make the same point only once?	_____	_____	_____
8. Do you make your points in the most convincing order?	_____	_____	_____
9. Is it clear what *action* the reader should take?	_____	_____	_____
10. Are the major points identified visually for the reader?	_____	_____	_____
11. Is it clear what point is being illustrated by each exhibit?	_____	_____	_____
12. Is your grammar correct? Does the memo read smoothly?	_____	_____	_____

Reader Guideline

Subject of the report or memo:

Name of the primary reader:

Question the reader might ask:

My position in relation to the primary reader:
  —professional:
  —personal:

How extensive is his or her knowledge of the subject?
  (great, minimal, nonexistent—describe)

What are his or her biases or preconceived ideas about the
  subject?

What are his or her significant managerial traits and stylistic
  preferences?

Who are the secondary readers?

Is anyone else likely to receive this report?

Primary and Secondary Source Checklist

Ask yourself these questions about your primary sources:

1. Does the source have a vested interest in the result of the study? Will the results directly affect him or her?

2. Does the source have a reputation for accuracy? (We know some managers whose gift for self-promotion tends to get in the way when they are providing information.)

Ask yourself these questions as you read your secondary sources:

1. Is the source objective? (Are there any obvious biases?)

2. Is the source up-to-date?

3. Are statistical sources comparable? (It may be impossible to use two sets of statistical data to support your argument because they were developed on the basis of different samples or used different methods. Check for this before you actually begin to write your report.)

Feasibility Checklist

1. Does existing technology support this proposal?

2. Will the people involved accept this change?
   —your superior
   —your peers
   —your subordinate

3. Can the organization's existing systems handle this change?
   —the personnel system
   —the control system

4. If the proposed solution has far-reaching implications, will it be accepted by
   —senior management
   —the public?

Grouping Form

Findings	Generalizations	Further Generalizations
_____		
_____	_____	
_____		_____
_____		
_____	_____	
_____		_____
_____		
_____	_____	
_____		_____
_____	_____	
_____		_____
_____		
_____	_____	
_____		_____
_____		
_____	_____	
_____		

Diagramming Checklist

1. Does the thesis sentence state your major point and nothing else?

2. Does each generalization include all the supporting statements and nothing else?

3. Are all the generalizations supported by at least two subpoints?

4. Are statements written in full declarative sentences (no questions, no phrases)?

5. For inductively ordered support—
   Do all points in support of a generalization relate to the generalization in the same way? (Are they all reasons, or steps, or parts of a whole?)

6. For deductively ordered support—
   Are the premises truly dependent? Do they lead unequivocably to your conclusion?

7. For both—
   Does the support for each generalization or assertion answer every question the reader might ask?

8. Did you consider the reader's needs when you chose the order?
   —picked a deductive order for a reader who is opposed to your thesis?
   —picked an inductive order for all other readers?

Guidelines for Setting a Writing Schedule

1. Establish the final deadline for the report.

2. Set your personal deadline two days earlier (nothing goes as quickly as you think it will).

3. Allow time to have the report typed. Add a day for proof-reading and corrections.

4. Set aside time for revising.

5. Divide the remaining time among problem solving, fact finding, organizing, and writing the first draft.

6. Set a timetable and stick to it.

Guidelines for Dictating

1. Use outlines to guide you.

2. Before you start the first paragraph, indicate what kind of communication it is—a memo, a letter, a long report? A draft or final copy? About how long? What kind of paper?

3. Dictate capitalization, punctuation, paragraphing. Spell out names, words that sound like other words, and words that have more than one spelling.

4. When you are making comments to the typist (corrections or instructions), be certain they are not confused with your text. We have all seen embarrassing asides that appeared in the final copy.

5. If you dictate afterthoughts at the end of a tape, leave written instructions about their insertion in the text.

6. Read and correct everything you dictate. Remember, the author, not the secretary, is responsible for the final copy.

7. Don't be afraid to dictate draft copy for later revision. Most secretaries would rather type from a tape than decipher an illegibly written draft.

First Draft Guidelines

1. Be natural.

2. Set up the reader's expectations.

3. Review and preview regularly.

4. Construct your paragraphs intelligently.

5. Don't make assertions unless you draw inferences from them.

6. Don't skip steps.

7. Elaborate on the unusual.

8. Use examples and be specific.

9. Stay with the diagram.

10. Keep writing.

Guide for Using Charts and Graphs

Message	Preferred Chart Form
Components of a whole	pie chart
Components of several wholes	bar chart
A ranking of items in one time period	bar chart
Comparison of several items in one time period	bar chart
Change over time of one or several variables	line graph
Comparison of change in several variables	dot chart

Exhibit Checklist

1. Does the exhibit clarify your argument for the reader?

2. Does the exhibit make one point, and one point only?

3. Does the title of the exhibit indicate its significance to the reader?

4. Does the exhibit accurately show relationships?

Writing Evaluation Checklist

1. Is it structurally sound?
   —is the thought logically developed?
   —do paragraphs and headings clearly reflect that development?
   —are there any constructions that don't make sense?
   —do the connecting phrases show correct relationships
   between ideas?

2. Does it answer all the questions it raises?

3. Is it concise?
   —does it tell the reader the facts he or she needs to know
   and no more?
   —are all unnecessary words and phrases deleted?

4. Is it appropriate in tone and language?
   —is the tone appropriate for the reader to whom it is
   aimed?
   —is the language adaped to the vocabulary of the reader?
   —are all technical terms and abbreviations explained?
   —is the writing free of sexist words or phrases?

5. Are there errors of grammar, spelling, or punctuation?

6. Summary evaluation: Is the memo or report effective? (Use
   the scale below.)

   Superior   Acceptable   Unacceptable

First Draft Guidelines

1. Be natural.

2. Set up the reader's expectations.

3. Review and preview regularly.

4. Construct your paragraphs intelligently.

5. Don't make assertions unless you draw inferences from them.

6. Don't skip steps.

7. Elaborate on the unusual.

8. Use examples and be specific.

9. Stay with the diagram.

10. Keep writing.

Guide for Using Charts and Graphs

Message	Preferred Chart Form
Components of a whole	pie chart
Components of several wholes	bar chart
A ranking of items in one time period	bar chart
Comparison of several items in one time period	bar chart
Change over time of one or several variables	line graph
Comparison of change in several variables	dot chart

Exhibit Checklist

1. Does the exhibit clarify your argument for the reader?

2. Does the exhibit make one point, and one point only?

3. Does the title of the exhibit indicate its significance to the reader?

4. Does the exhibit accurately show relationships?

Writing Evaluation Checklist

1. Is it structurally sound?
   —is the thought logically developed?
   —do paragraphs and headings clearly reflect that development?
   —are there any constructions that don't make sense?
   —do the connecting phrases show correct relationships
   between ideas?

2. Does it answer all the questions it raises?

3. Is it concise?
   —does it tell the reader the facts he or she needs to know
   and no more?
   —are all unnecessary words and phrases deleted?

4. Is it appropriate in tone and language?
   —is the tone appropriate for the reader to whom it is
   aimed?
   —is the language adaped to the vocabulary of the reader?
   —are all technical terms and abbreviations explained?
   —is the writing free of sexist words or phrases?

5. Are there errors of grammar, spelling, or punctuation?

6. Summary evaluation: Is the memo or report effective? (Use
   the scale below.)

   Superior   Acceptable   Unacceptable